THE RED SECT

Enzo Martucci

Edited by Kevin I. Slaughter

STAND ALONE

Published by Union of Egoists and
Underworld Amusements
ISBN: 978-1-943687-10-7
STAND ALONE SA1257
First edition, September 2023.

Originally published as *La Setta Rosa* in 1953.
English translation ©2023 Kevin I. Slaughter.
Editing & design by Kevin I. Slaughter.
Copyediting assistance by Alex Kies.

This is the first English-language translation of Enzo
Martucci's book. Where Martucci quotes non-Italian-
language authors such as Max Stirner, Fyodor Dostoyevsky,
and the works of Marx and Engels, pre-existing English-
language translations have been used as cited in footnotes.

Footnotes are by the editor unless appended with [ENZO],
then they are by the author.

This book is part of the *Stand Alone* series by the Union of
Egoists. *Stand Alone* is mixed medium and format journal
produced at irregular intervals. The focus is Egoism and
the individuals associated with it.

More information:
www.UnionOfEgoists.com
www.UndeworldAmusements.com

CONTENTS

PREFACE

There are two types of anticommunism: bourgeois and anarchist.

The first is crude, foolish, and reactionary. It is a retrogressive attitude dictated by the need to preserve, at any cost, the fear of God and the priest's prerogative, the submissiveness of the people, and the privilege of capital.

It is a curious mixture in which the most disparate elements are gathered, ranging from the Syllabus to Masonic principles, from liberal economics to Saragat's *dirigisme*.[1] And all this has no other basis than *fear*, which drives impossible combinations, unnatural alliances, in the quest to avoid the threat of a revolution that, while leaving the very substance of gregarious life unchanged, would achieve the much-reviled *change of guard* in the command posts

---

1   Giuseppe Saragat was a Italian democratic socialist politician who, at the time of the writing, was founder and leader of the Italian Democratic Socialist Party. Saragat later served as the president of Italy from 1964 to 1971. *Dirigisme* is an economic policy characterized by strong government intervention in a nation's economy, often involving extensive regulation and planning. It's a system where the government plays a central role in guiding and coordinating economic activity.

and Pluto's coffers.

Anarchist anticommunism, on the other hand, is very different. It is the expression of a strongly individualistic sentiment that rebels against the hypocrisies and shackles of the current world but, at the same time, seeks to prevent the advent of a worse future and the rigid regimentation of men in the bureaucratic-industrial barracks of Stalinist society. For this reason, anarchist anticommunism is hated by everyone, and the publication of this book has been hindered in various ways by people who today profess to be fiercely anti-Bolshevik but yesterday, when their interests coincided, took power with the Kremlin's servants. People who, with Togliatti, would still find an agreement but will never forgive me for the anti-theological and anticlerical campaign carried out in Italy in the years 1945–47 and the successes achieved in the numerous debates supported by the big guns of Catholic propaganda.

Thus, due to the insidious action of powerful enemies, no publisher would have dared to publish *The Red Sect*, and it would have remained as a manuscript on my desk if a personal friend, the architect Vittorio Verrocchio, who is not an anarchist but has a generous heart and a free and original spirit, had not provided me with the means to have the book printed. Fortunately, it appears at a time when the Bolshevik Hydra becomes more insidious, subtle, and penetrating, and therefore more dangerous.

In fact, the *détente* maneuver initiated by Malenkov, after Stalin's death, aims at nothing but avoiding the risk of a hot war for Russia and disarming the West morally and materially to conquer it more easily. The successor to the modern Genghis Khan is a sly fox but does not have the prestige that the deceased dictator possessed and, therefore, cannot feel safe to be followed by all the communists in the world in the likely event that the Cold War turns into an armed conflict. And to buy the time needed to consolidate his power in the Soviet republic and the satellite states, he abandons Stalin's rigid and brutal policy and pretends to want to ease tensions in the East and seek means to reach peace with the governments beyond the Iron Curtain. In this way, he hopes to obtain a few years of peace during which he will increase his authority and establish a power similar to that of his predecessor, while the Western bloc crumbles under the Moscow threat.

Indeed, the European countries that had decided to unite and arm themselves to defend against the aggression of red Pan-Slavism, when they see that the danger fades away, will not remain in the Atlantic Pact only to serve the interests of conservative American and British imperialism. Gradually, they will separate and demobilize their armies and war industries; the contrasts and rivalries among national capitalisms will manifest themselves anew, with increased vigor, and will put peoples against each other in the name of the claims that each advances.

Meanwhile, in order to progressively weaken each country from within, communist fifth columns will intensify sabotage of production, strikes and agitations, and disruption of the economy. The masses will become increasingly infatuated with Russia, and even many elements of the liberal bourgeoisie will look at it with tenderness when it does not present itself with the face of Stalin's tyrannical and conquering dictatorship, but with the appearance of Malenkov's republican, democratic, and pacifist visage.

And finally, once the natural maturation has occurred, Russia, which, despite the play it has performed, will remain dictatorial internally and warmongering externally, will throw itself with its formidable army, constantly reinforced, on the divided and discordant Western enemies and will bring them down one by one. Thus, instead of the plan organized for the destruction of Bolshevism by American high finance and its clerico-bourgeois allies in Europe, the opposite plan, astutely conceived and implemented by the red fox who has sat on Stalin's imperial throne, poisoning in time the rival to the succession, Zhdanov,[2] will be realized.

Moreover, the fact that communism remains what it was is demonstrated by the recent events in Czechoslovakia and East Germany. In the former country, a terrible police reaction has unleashed against the miners who, driven by desperation, were striking for an improvement in their precarious economic and political condition. And, after a few days,

---

2   Andrei Zhdanov (1896–1948) was a Soviet politician and chief propagandist in the 1940s. He developed the Zhdanov Doctrine, the Soviet Union's cultural policy.

in Berlin, Russian soldiers ruthlessly shot at the working masses who were demanding bread and freedom. This is the loosening of the brakes promised by Mr. Malenkov. And this is the Soviet paradise in which proletarians receive lead in their bellies.

Therefore, faced with the increased threat of the Bolshevik Leviathan, I am proud to publish this book, which is a challenge to it. And I hope that it can help to push free men—if there are still any left—towards a more decisive attitude of resistance to red totalitarianism and any other authoritarian form, differently colored but equally harmful to the freedom of individuals and the expansion of life.

ENZO MARTUCCI
Pescara, July 1953.

KILLING
THE SOUL

On a cold and foggy November day in 1923, I met the Hungarian communist Stefano Kolnar in a café on Place du Combat in Paris.[3] He recognized me immediately and came towards me with his hand outstretched.

"It's been three years since we last saw each other," he observed as he sat down beside me. "Do you remember when we were together in Genoa? How well the police treated us then and how comforting the guard at the Doge's Palace was. My bones are still sore from the beating...."

I smiled, recalling the dark and fetid cell of the Tower where Kolnar and I, who had met in Milan at Malatesta's house and were reunited in Genoa, had been imprisoned. He had fled his homeland after the fall of Bela Kun and feared that the Italian government would hand him over to Horthy. Instead, I saw him before me, free and healthy, in Paris.

"I'm glad they didn't send you to Hungary," I said. "When we were released, we took care of you,

---

3   Later renamed *Place du Colonel Fabien* after the communist resistance fighter Pierre Georges.

but the lawyer who came to the police station on our behalf to request your release was told by the authorities that you would be expelled from Italy but not handed over to your country. But I was afraid they wouldn't keep their promise."

"They kept it," Kolnar replied. "After three months in Marassi, two guardian angels "accompanied me to the Swiss border and left me in the hands of the Swiss *gendarmes*. Then even the land of William Tell didn't want me, and I went to Vienna. But what a life, my friend, and how many struggles in these years..."

He began to tell me the adventures of his stormy life as an international agitator when a beautiful young woman with languid and fascinating eyes approached our table and spoke to Stefano in an unknown language. I looked at her, struck by her elegance, the statuesque perfection of her body, and the voluptuous gaze that troubled my senses as a passionate young man. Around us, in the small, smoky café, there were only proletarians in worn-out clothes and *lavallière* ties, with worn-out and poorly dressed women. That *mademoiselle* who seemed like a high-class *cocotte* or an aristocratic damsel contrasted with the environment, and it was unclear how she had ended up there, among Italian and Spanish exiles.

"Do you like her?" Stefano asked as the girl sat down beside him. "It's Vanda, my lover, a bourgeois daughter I met in Budapest when I was at university. Then I had to flee, and her family forced her to marry an industrialist. Last year we met again in Vienna, and she left her husband and came with me. She even helped me financially, and I owe her money if I managed to escape the clutches of the Austrian police. I regret not being able to introduce her because she doesn't speak Italian and blasphemes in French."

I looked at the girl who smiled at me.

"You must love her very much," I observed, "if she has left her family and comfort to share your agitated and dangerous life with you."

"Yes, she loves me," replied Stefano. "These foolish women do nothing but love. Especially women of her class. They don't care about politics, they don't concern themselves with the condition of the proletariat, and they only think about the man they go to bed with. But this one has been very useful to me. And she will be even more useful in the future. She is only twenty years old, beautiful, clever, and obeys everything I command. For me, you see, this sex fiend would throw herself into the fire. And I use her for my theories. In a few days, I will send her to Hungary to deliver material to my comrades."

"What?" I exclaimed indignantly. "Do you want to expose the woman who loves you and has ruined herself for you to such a grave danger? Don't you think that the Hungarian police certainly know she is your friend and will arrest her as soon as she sets foot back in her country? If they find the material on her, she will spend many years in prison. And you want to make her run this risk?"

Stefano became annoyed. "What do you want me to do then?" he asked brusquely. "I can't go back because I'm too well known. I don't have any other trusted people at the moment. The comrades need what Vanda has to deliver right away. So it is necessary for her to go."

"No," I replied, getting heated. "You shouldn't send her because it would be an infamy to push a poor girl who has already given you so many proofs of her affection into prison. Besides, she's not a communist, you said so yourself. She's a woman who lives only for love, and if she plunges into the abyss, it's to please you. How can you expect her to sacrifice herself for an idea she doesn't feel? How can you accept such a monstrous sacrifice?"

"But I feel the theory, and I take advantage of the love this woman has for me to serve the cause. Any means are good as long as they allow me to achieve my goal."

"Forget this most loathsome Machiavellianism and answer my question instead: if it's really necessary for the material to be delivered, why don't you try your luck and return to your country clandestinely instead of exposing Vanda?"

"Because they would probably arrest me, and I'm more useful outside than inside."

"Here's the usual excuse of the communists, who typify 'all bark and no bite.'[4] You always avoid facing responsibilities and unload them onto the shoulders of women, young people, and the unconscious, those

_____

4   The original phrase "*armiamoci e partite*" is an Italian proverb meaning to "arm up and run", a derisive and mocking accusation meaning someone who talks big and does nothing.

whom you use as blind instruments. But why don't you step forward instead of pushing others?"

The Hungarian's eyes flashed. The girl, who was listening without understanding our conversation, which was in Italian, turned her curious gaze from Stefano to me.

"I," roared the Bolshevik, "have never backed down, and I never will. I have devoted my life to the social revolution, and I am ready to die for it. But today, it is necessary to spare myself from skirmishes in order to prepare for the great and final battle in which I will fall, seeing the victory of the proletariat."

"Meanwhile, let others fall in the skirmishes. And who will be sacrificed? A woman: your lover. How can you bear the thought that, while you roam the streets, this girl who loved you, who intoxicated you with her caresses and held you in her arms, will moan for you, because of you, in the cell of a penitentiary? Ah! Stefano, you are really devoid of feelings..."

"Of course, I am not sentimental like you anarchists. Your character is ridiculously romantic; mine, that of us communists, is scientific and rationalist. My intelligence indicates the goal to be reached and the means to be used. And I use them with cold, inexorable logic, ignorant of the weaknesses that you would like me to have."

"But you have no soul," I shouted in his face.

The Bolshevik smirked with superiority.

"Yes, you're right," he replied. "I have no soul: we communists don't have it. And we'll make you lose it too. Our goal is to *kill the soul.*"

MARXISTS ON TRIAL

Stefano Kolnar was telling the truth. Communism wants to kill the soul. Bolshevik education suffocates all feelings in man and replaces them with blind fanaticism. Love, friendship, pity, passions do not exist in the communist; he has cut them off, destroyed his human essence, made a void within himself and filled it with the monstrous idea that dominates, alone and unchallenged. A slave to this idea, he wants to impose it on others and wants them to accept it as he has, without discussing, without evaluating, without subjecting it to the critical examination of intelligence. Dogmatic and sectarian, he attacks those who do not allow themselves to be converted. Whoever rejects the Marxist gospel and touches it with doubt is a heretic who must be fought with the same means the Church used in the Middle Ages to suffocate heresy. Whoever does not enter the red barracks or does not want to undergo their degrading discipline is an *enemy of the proletariat* or a *traitor*. Against these, the communist uses all weapons: when he can, he takes up his pistol as a GPU agent and shoots them in the back of the head; and when he cannot resort to violence, he uses slander, lies, and systematic cowardice.

He has learned from Machiavelli and the Jesuits that the end justifies the means and does not shy away from the most disgusting and repugnant acts in order to achieve his goal. Fanaticized by the cause to which he dedicates himself completely, he is ruthless towards others and does not hesitate to sacrifice them in the interest of the *ideal*. If he has to push his wife into prostitution or ruin a friend or send a fellow fighter to jail to serve the party, he does it immediately without a moment's hesitation. Stalin denounced his political friends to the Tsarist police and had them arrested, thinking that their hatred against the state would increase in prison.

In exile, I met a Tuscan communist who offered his young and attractive wife to corrupt a public security agent and obtain the clandestine transmission of letters between him and his superiors.

The Bolshevik has no heart, no soul, no feelings, he is below the brute which instinctively shies away from certain acts, while he does not shy away from anything and transcends any abjection that the advantage of the sect requires.

Bent by strict discipline, he renounces his personal freedom in the hands of his superiors and obediently follows all their orders. There is no infamy he would not commit, no humiliation he would not endure if his leaders commanded him to. A zealous follower, he obeys without discussion, he obeys solicitously even if they tell him he must be sodomized or

ENZO MARTUCCI

that he must accompany his daughter to the brothel.

The interest of the ideal requires this passive submission and he bends his back and serves with pleasure, waiting to take revenge when Bolshevism triumphs and each of its followers can indulge their own lust for dominance, tyrannizing non-communists. Therefore, his fanaticism is not at all disinterested because he does not devote himself to an idea solely for the purpose of achieving justice or equality; rather, he dedicates himself to Bolshevism and lives only for it, hoping that the proletarian dictatorship will allow him to enjoy nationalized wealth and exercise authority, great or small, in society, depending on his rank in the party hierarchy. Whether a people's commissar or a Red Guard, a torturer in prisons or an executioner at Lubianka, the communist wants to be a big shot and crush someone else under his own heel. Meanwhile, the heels of the leaders crush his chest and he endures it, disciplined and satisfied, because only in this way can the *idea* triumph and he can put a braided cap on his head.

The high and mighty leaders of the world revolution, together with their arrogant generals, hone their skills for the impending despotism by treating the faithful soldiers as mere slaves and subjecting them to various menial tasks. One of these big shots, a political exile confined to the island of Ponza, would recline in a beach chair and enjoy being fanned for hours on end by two young communist exiles, the B... sisters. He acted as a sultan in his harem, amidst the odalisques... And yet, no one delivered a swift kick in the ass to that deserter of the land.

Another leader who systematically appropriated the shares that the underlings paid for the Red Aid demanded that his comrades send their wives and sisters home to him.

The comrades obeyed, honored by the general's condescension, who after giving the women a lesson in sex education, taught the men history, that Zarathustra was a Carthaginian leader who came to Italy with Hannibal and was killed by the Romans at the Battle of Zama.

Occasionally, among the fatherly communist figures, one meets an educated person like the hunchbacked Gramsci, the Torquemada of Italian Bolshevism; but generally, the red leaders, whose ignorance is surpassed only by their presumption, are poor in spirit. Professor Torelli (of what?) confused the thought of Kant with that of Gentile; and when I demonstrated to him that Kantian critical idealism is quite different from Gentile's absolute idealism, because for the former, there is the *noumenon*, the thing in itself, which we know only phenomenally, while for the latter there is only the human spirit that posits things, and he—the professor of bestiality—answered, with a smile of the superman, that I did not understand philosophy.

The Turin-born Roveda argued to a twenty-eight-year-old that there is historical evidence of the practice of sexual promiscuity in primitive societies. I replied that this evidence is lacking and that he was taking simple inductions from some writers who believed that certain customs of modern barbarians, such as offering a wife to a guest among the Eskimos, and certain historical customs, such as the sacred prostitutes of the Babylonians, the *jus primae noctis*, and the sacred defloration in Cambodia, were survivals of an ancient promiscuity. Roveda, not knowing what to say, turned his back and walked away indignantly. In reality, he did not know what the asserters of erotic communism of primitive times had written, who used arguments much more serious than his foolish sentences. He had never read Bachofen, McLennan, Lubbock, Morgan, Giraud-Teulon, and was ignorant of what Westermarck, Darwin, and Wundt had contrarily argued. Roveda had only read *The Origin of the Family, Private Property and the State*, the book in which Engels, copying Morgan, asserts, for the purposes of historical materialism, that in primeval humanity there existed the common possession of women, and that only when man formed a property did he want a woman solely for himself and imposed fidelity on her in order to transmit the goods to his own offspring. However, Roveda was ignorant of what other writers had opposed to his idol Engels; thus, with haughty confidence, he declared that there is historical evidence of promiscuity.

The same masters of Marxism, the luminaries of Bolshevik science, have also made absurd statements more than once.

Giovanni Gentile in his book *The Philosophy of Marx* observes that Engels has confused the Hegelian idea immanent in things with the Platonic idea of its transcendent nature. Engels in fact wrote in *Anti-Dühring*:

"Hegel was an idealist, that is, for him the ideas in his head were not already the more or less abstract images of real things and events, but on the contrary for him things and their development were only the actualized images of the idea which already exists, before the world, somewhere."

This passage shows how well Engels understood Hegelian philosophy.

Karl Marx, who taught his disciples the art of calumny, wrote a book against Stirner entitled with an ironic motto: *The Saint Max*.[5] In this book, the communist pope presents the author of *The Ego and His Own* as a metaphysician without knowledge, a weak imitator of Hegel, a philosopher of the German petty bourgeoisie, a "sentimental braggart" in theory, and a reactionary in practice.

In reality, Stirner's intelligence was superior to Marx's, and his spirit much more revolutionary. Stirner is, in history, the true anarchist philosopher, the only one who deserves this name.

Proudhon, Bakunin, Kropotkin, Réclus, are nothing but semi-anarchists, representatives of a compromise between individualism and collectivism, between socialism and anarchism. Theirs is only the anarchy of Paolo Gille,[6] the anarchy with disci-

---

5   *The German Ideology* is a posthumous collection of writings by Marx and Engels, published in 1932. An excerpt of the third section was published in Italy in 1903 under the name *Il Santo Max*.

6   Paolo Gille, *Abbozzo di una filosofia della dignità*

pline, the limited freedom of the individual who is no longer subject to the state but must subordinate himself to society for the satisfaction of his complete needs, and must always agree with everyone. In essence, they deny the state but deify society, as noted by Palante;[7] and they propose, against those who violate the future harmony, the harshest sanctions ranging from public contempt and general alienation, as advised by Kropotkin in *The Conquest of Bread*, to incarceration in the mental institution advocated by Malatesta in his pamphlet *Anarchy*.

Stirner, instead, is more logical as an anarchist. He believes that the individual is the only reality above which there is nothing else. Thereforehe wants the individual to fully realize themselves and satisfy their egoism, freeing themselves from their conceptions of the sanctity and inviolability of their limitations. God, morality, humanity, society, nation, and state are only ghosts oppressing the ego because it has created, respects, and serves them. But when the ego destroys them, when it makes them return to nothingness, then, having been freed from every spiritual and material tie, it will be able to live as it pleases, freely cooperating with its peers or fighting against them, depending on the needs, feelings, and interests that prevail in it at different times. It will be the *bellum omnium contra omnes*, tempered by individual alliances; but it will also be the natural freedom in

umana (Outline of a Philosophy of Human Dignity).

7   Georges Palante, *La sensibilità individualista* (The Individualist Sensibility).

which the individual can try to assert themselves by any means.

These are Stirner's ideas that can be accepted or fought against, but not falsified. One can believe with Basch that the individualist philosopher was antisocial and a disorganizer of the ties that unite human beings, or one can see in him the theorist of voluntary and spontaneous association that does not absorb the individual, does not pretend to eternalize itself, and does not deny the contrasts and struggles among the *unique*, strong, and independent. But one cannot claim that Stirner is a bourgeois philosopher when his philosophy constitutes the most radical subversion of the historical conception of life.

Stirner, the forerunner of Nietzsche, exalted egoism, pushed man beyond good and evil, and claimed the right to satisfy all personal passions, good and bad.

On the other hand, the communists want to suppress good passions and enhance bad ones: fanaticism, intolerance, cruelty, thirst for power. Their amorality, therefore, is to Stirner's amorality what the hypocritical perfidy of the snake is to the straightforward aggressiveness of the lion.

Stirner was an opponent of communism. "By the abolition of all personal property," he wrote, "[Communism] only presses me back still more into dependence on another, viz., on the generality or collectivity; and, loudly as it always attacks the 'State,' what it intends is itself again a State, a status, a condition hindering my free movement, a sovereign power over me. Communism rightly revolts against the pressure that I experience from individual proprietors; but still more horrible is the might that it puts in the hands of the collectivity."[8]

Marx opposed Stirner to better assert his doctrine and, as was his habit, resorted to slander, lies, and ridicule. However, what he wrote in *The Saint Max* is no more valuable than Torelli's confusion between Kant and Gentile and Engels' identification of the Hegelian idea with the Platonic one. And if the master, who had wit and culture, so often falsified the thought of others in bad faith, the disciples, who combine bad faith with ignorance, must necessarily arrive at the conclusion the Bolshevik whitewasher, police confidant, and sisters' pimp reached in his speeches:

"In communism is our salvation. Everything that is not communist must be rejected, opposed, denigrated."

---

8   Max Stirner, translated by Steven T. Byington, *The Ego and His Own,* New York: Benjamin R. Tucker 1907.

WHAT IS MARXISM

But what is Marxist communism, this *Good Book* preached by the Jew from Trier[9] and blindly accepted by dissatisfied manual workers who dream of becoming commissars?

Marxism is a theory based on historical materialism, which sees economic factors as the absolute that determines, *a priori*, the facts and binds them in the succession of a predetermined order that inevitably culminates in a classless society.

A reversal of Hegelianism, it replaces Hegel's absolute idea with material need; and this material need, this economic need, creates history, anticipates its development and leads it, through the progressive contradiction of interests, to the annihilation of all contradictions and universal well-being. Man is nothing but a puppet without will, a slave to the cramps of hunger that force him to think and act in a certain way, to follow a marked path and to reach, after predetermined struggles and conflicts, an inevitable goal. And history, which follows the obligatory

9   Karl Marx.

rails of materialistic fatalism, can never change direction but must pass through the regulatory stations and necessarily stop at the last of them.

"In the social production of their existence, men inevitably enter into definite relations, which are independent of their will, namely relations of production appropriate to a given stage in the development of their material forces of production. The totality of these relations of production constitutes the economic structure of society, the real foundation, on which arises a legal and political superstructure and to which correspond definite forms of social consciousness. The mode of production of material life conditions the general process of social, political and intellectual life. It is not the consciousness of men that determines their existence, but their social existence that determines their consciousness."[10]

In this way, historical materialism denies any role to moral force in determining human events. Feelings, will, ideals have no intrinsic efficacy, no real influence in life, but are only illusory appearances of a material determinism over which they exert no action. It is economic interest that guides the world, and men are reduced to mere pawns moved by the irresistible impetus of this material interest to which they cannot react.

But reality is very different from how Marx represents it. Man certainly has economic needs, but he also has emotional, ideal, and passionate needs, and

---

10   Karl Marx, *A Contribution to the Critique of Political Economy,* Progress Publishers, Moscow, 1977

just as the former act on the latter, so these act on the former. Often, a person carries out their activities in accordance with their own material interest and forms ideas that correspond to that interest; but when a spontaneous idea flashes through their mind or a fiery passion is unleashed in their heart, they undergo the influence of these moral forces and subordinate or sacrifice their material interest to them.

"Man everywhere and at all times," explained Dostoevsky, "whoever he may be, has preferred to act as he chose and not in the least as his reason and advantage dictated. And one may choose what is contrary to one's own interests, and sometimes one *positively ought* (that is my idea). One's own free unfettered choice, one's own caprice, however wild it may be, one's own fancy worked up at times to frenzy—is that very 'most advantageous advantage' which we have overlooked, which comes under no classification and against which all systems and theories are continually being shattered to atoms. And how do these wiseacres know that man wants a normal, a virtuous choice? What has made them conceive that man must want a rationally advantageous choice? What man wants is simply independent choice, whatever that independence may cost and wherever it may lead."[11]

Marxists will object that such cases are pathological, individual, but that social life is always determined by material interests and the conflicts that

---

11   Fyodor Dostoyevsky, translated by Constance Garnett, *Notes from Underground*, London: Heinemann, 1918.

ENZO MARTUCCI

arise among them. However, it is not uncommon in history to see groups, masses, and peoples driven by an idea or a feeling, sometimes even by absurdity or madness, neglecting their material interests and acting against them, to the advantage of the spiritual interest they felt most strongly. Human egoism is not simply materialistic, it does not only aim at satisfying the belly, but tends to satisfy all the physical and psychic needs of man; and when the latter prevail over the former, he satisfies them to the detriment of bodily well-being and comfort. If this were not the case, we could not explain the sight of the great lord Bakunin chained in the cell of Alessio, Prince Kropotkin as a revolutionary agitator in Europe, Count Tolstoy as a peasant in the steppe. We could not understand Paul of Tarsus and Francis of Assisi, Carlo Pisacane and Cesare Battisti, and we would have to see the typical representatives of humanity and its healthy and normal action in the bloated capitalist exploiter and the striking worker demanding a salary increase. Man is man and not a pig, and even when he rebels against every ethical constraint and every social law for the complete affirmation of the self, he professes the heroic and Dionysian egoism of Nietzsche or the romantic and negating egoism of Stirner, but not the ignoble belly-fetishism of Pantagruel.

As Elisée Réclus wrote, "It is the sap that makes the tree; it is ideas that make society. No historical fact is better established than this." [12]

---

12   Élisée Réclus, *Évolution et Révolution* (Evolution and Revolution), Paris: La Révolte, 1891.

Therefore, contrary to what Engels asserted, the determining causes of this or that social metamorphosis or revolution must be sought not so much in the metamorphoses of production and exchange as in the heads and hearts of men.

Christianity and the Crusades, the Reformation and the French Revolution, were more the work of idea and feeling than of material interests.

Then there is an ancient idea that has deeply engraved itself into humanity, causing wars, revolutions, delusions, fanaticisms, and has influenced customs, modified the conditions of social existence, and had an enormously impacts all lives throughout history: this is the idea of God.

Well, it originally arose from a need of the spirit that economic necessity could not explain. If we adhere to the materialist and positivist method, that is, the method of the Marxists, we must believe that the divine idea was born in primitive man as a result of the incomprehension of natural phenomena (lightning, thunder, hail, earthquake), and the fear of death. Therefore, God was created by our distant ancestors to satisfy a psychological need that material interests or modes of production could not influence. Whether fruitarian or carnivorous, better or worse nourished, with a stone axe or an iron spear, associated in a herd or living in a family, whatever the conditions of his material existence, the savage of prehistory would always have felt the terror of the end and would have imagined that the cause of a lightning bolt or hurricane was an invisible being more powerful than him.

Later, material interests crystallized around this idea because some men wanted others to believe them to be Representatives of God on earth, in order to derive wealth and privileges from it. But at the beginning, at the origins, no economic cause could operate on the emergence of religious belief. God was born of the torments of the soul, not of the cramps of hunger.

It is not true, therefore, that man is and has always been determined solely by economic factors, which in Marxist philosophy is what the idea is in Hegelian philosophy. If there were no different factors acting on us, if everything reduced to an absolute from which everything derives, if material and ideal and sentimental life were identified in the indistinct unity of an inconceivable monism, then this immanent absolute, this unique whole, could not be called an economic factor.

We distinguish and identify various aspects of reality by their peculiar characteristics. We recognize the color red through its difference from blue and green, and we identify economic facts through their specific nature, which gives them their own physiognomy and prevents them from being confused with non-economic facts. But if reality is undifferentiated, if the beating of the heart and the flash of intelligence, the passion for an idea and the struggle for food, are various manifestations of the same material need that determines humans in thought and practical activity, then this single need cannot be identified with any of its forms. It cannot be said, that is, that it is economic because it will also be spiritual, ideological, and sentimental, just as a person is not only a head but also a body, a thought, a sensitivity, etc. Without any distinct and autonomous natures, the only absolute nature will not involve distinctions; it will have all attributes and qualities and will be, at the same time, economic and ideal, sentimental and emotional. So how can it be said that it is economic and that, as such, it influences the intellect and feeling when they will form one and the same thing with the economy? The absolute has no name, and Marx, to be consistent, should not say that man is determined by economic need but by the absolute.

But Marx and Marxists argue that economic need is not absolute like the Hegelian idea but rather relative. This means that outside of what is economic, there is something else that is not economic and that has its own nature and autonomous life. So why, always and in all cases, should the economic determine the non-economic and never be determined by it? Why will there be no reciprocity of influences but rather conditions of dependence of one element on the other?

Marx wants the relative to play the part of the absolute. He asserts that economic need governs all others, forcing man to act always in a certain way, that is, in accordance with his material interests, and prearranges future action and the concatenation of events that determines them *a priori*. But if Marx were consistent with his premise about the relativity of the economic, he would recognize that the relative cannot become absolute, that material interest influences other interests but is also influenced by them, that social existence sometimes determines consciousness, but at other times it is consciousness that determines social existence.

He would then come to the conclusion that man, torn by different and opposing tendencies, by conflicting interests, acts in various ways and that therefore, in history, new elements always arise that change the orientation, the general direction; that facts are not determinable *a priori* but knowable *a posteriori*, and that humanity is not necessarily headed towards a predetermined goal, the final communism, but continuously changes its goal and never stops.

But if Marx and the Marxists were to admit this, they would have to give up historical materialism. And without this foundation, communism would no longer be the inevitable reality of the future.

COMMUNIST UTOPIA

The dialectical process of history leads to communism, as Marx teaches. The series of economic contradictions ends in the annihilation of all contradictions. Class warfare and conflict of interests lead to the disappearance of classes and the reconciliation of interests in socialist society. Universal harmony is the ultimate goal of social evolution.

But why is this so? Why must peace arise from struggle, agreement from conflict, and synthesis from the opposition of thesis and antithesis? Couldn't it be that the struggle would remain eternal and that humanity would struggle until the day of death with the torments of economic and other types of conflicts?

Marxism is fatalistic. Practice is voluntaristic. Human will creates history but creates it by fighting against the will of other humans who do not give in to defeat and return to the fray. The human tragedy, born with Adam or the Peking Man, will persist until the last man. Eden will remain the fantasy of daydreaming sociologists who escape reality to take refuge in illusion.

Therefore, past utopias were, in a sense, also voluntaristic. The cities of the sun were an *ideal*, a goal that the will set for itself and sought to achieve. Plato and Campanella, Herzen and Bakunin took into account man, his feelings, his desires. Marxism instead asserts that social harmony is the fatal product of history, the extreme point to which we will arrive as a result of economic determinism and independently of human will. It is not understood, then, why communists strive to realize their society by any means when they could contemplate their navels and wait for the ripe pear to fall of its own accord.

Communism demonstrates that the concentration of capital and the conflict of interests between the bourgeoisie and the proletariat will lead the latter to expropriate the former and to nationalize the means of production. The super-powerful proletarian state, invested with all authority and functions, will prepare the necessary conditions for its own suppression. When these conditions are met, the proletarian state, like the classes, will disappear; and from state economy, we will move to social economy, *i.e.*, to the socialization of the means of production, their possession and use by the associated producing individuals, and the common consumption of the fruits of collective labor. From socialism, we will move to communism, from the formula "to each according to his merit" to the other "to each according to his needs, from each according to his abilities." It will be, in a word, the stateless communism of Bakunin,

Kropotkin, and Malatesta; only they wanted to reach it directly, through the immediate abolition of the state and property; Marx and his followers want to reach it through the centralizing state and the dictatorship of the proletariat.

But this is precisely the crux of the matter. Can the Bolshevik State destroy the classes and prevent new ones from emerging, thus achieving economic equality among individuals who, having reached parity in wealth and work, will do without government direction and will support each other in a communal and communist manner? Marx and his disciples answer yes. I believe the opposite. Because, assuming human selfishness and the invincible need that the individual feels to prevail over others, it would result in those proletarians who would be at the head of the State and should administer wealth in the public interest, ending up using it as their personal property, taking advantage of the authority that would consecrate them, the laws they would promulgate, and the bayonets that would support them. State property would become practically the property of the people's commissars, the arrogant officials, and the bigwigs of the Marxist world; and a new privileged class would be formed that would hold wealth and power and exploit and oppress the majority of the proletariat. The red thugs would like to keep for themselves, land, villas, and palaces, and show off luxury and make others work for them, not only for the material enjoyment of all this, but also to distinguish themselves and assert their superiority over the factory worker and the humble peasant. What happened in Russia would happen, where Stalin and his lackeys have control over everything, the lives of the subjects and bourgeois opulence; where a caste of rapacious *parvenus* feeds on the blood of workers, forces them to produce until physical exhaustion, and exploits them excessively in a slave-like manner. Those who protest, who demand more humane treatment, receive bullets in their stomachs from the police rifles or, in the best-case scenario, end up in forced labor in Siberia. And the communist state, the famous proletarian state, is nothing more than the despotic, bureaucratic police state that rehabilitates the deceased Tsarism.

The Marxist method does not therefore lead to the suppression of classes and economic equality, but creates a new predatory class, instead of the overthrown one, and exacerbates social inequalities. Nor, on the other hand, would immediate socialization, direct communism without the prelude of statization, even lead to perfect leveling and complete equality among collectivized individuals.

Assuming it were possible to realize Kropotkin's libertarian communism, there would remain within the new society many people who would not be satisfied with giving according to their abilities and taking according to their needs, but would want to live their own way, try other experiences, create other social forms. They would not be satisfied with eating, drinking, having fun, and working with the community for a few hours and dedicating the others to conformist personal inclinations influenced by the environment. They would not want to be like everyone else and do what everyone else would do. Collective ownership of every material good and common consumption would also exasperate them, even if it were the source of abundance and general well-being. They would cry out that man is not made for the life of an ant or a beehive, that mammals differ from insects and that the human being, even when he has destroyed the chains of private property, sacred and inviolable, and of the State that protects it, seeks to realize different ways of life, opposing forms that sometimes tolerate or help each other, but other times clash against each other.

Instead, the stateless communist society, *i.e.*, the society that Marx wants to reach through the dictatorship of the proletariat and to which Kropotkin believes it is possible to reach directly through revolution, can only be conceived as an immense flock of sheep, tied together and always forced to move together. And the bond that would keep the sheep united is conceivable only as a common flock spirit, that spirit that is at the bottom of our nature, which man inherited from the sociable chimpanzee from which, according to Kropotkin, he descends, and which only the abnormal and unnatural conditions created by past and present society have been able to attenuate, arousing differences, oppositions, and struggles among human individuals. But when the present society collapses and the degenerating influence it exerts on men disappears definitively, then, as a result of the new conditions (imposed by force by the dictatorship of the proletariat, according to Marx, or voluntarily accepted by sociable individuals, according to Kropotkin), the flock spirit will awaken and become stronger, the common human essence will prevail over personal originality and finally destroy it. Therefore, the most absolute monism and conformity will be established in humanity, everyone will spontaneously accept a single social and economic system, communism, and follow the same norm of thought and the same rule of conduct. There will no longer be a need for the State and laws that force, when everyone wants the same thing and acts equally. The last rare and pathological individual revolts will be suffocated by the unanimous mass, and the heavy grayness of triumphant gregariousness will build, on the corpses of the now destroyed personalities, the new and grotesque type of *collective man*.

Fortunately, this aspiration of communism is destined to remain eternally unrealized because, by nature, man is not all of one piece, not all a *herd animal*. Instead, it is a contradictory being, with social and antisocial tendencies and needs that will be preserved in every form of life. Therefore, Marxism will not result in universal sheep-like behavior, but practically, it will not go beyond Stalinism, which, instead of the indistinct classless and stateless multitude, creates a new elephantine State, despotically ruled by a class of *parvenus*, cruel and rapacious. And if Kropotkinism is ever realized, it will lead to the autonomous Commune in which the norm of conduct will not be established by unanimity of consent, but rather by the will of the majority deceived by demagogues and swindlers. Naturally, this majority, reunited in the Areopagus, will ostracize those who do not conform to its way of life. And everything will go as in the Greek city and in the medieval Commune where the strongest faction oppressed and banished the other enemy.

However, since conflicts, rivalries, and wars would inevitably arise among autonomous communes, to avoid these disasters, they will be federated. And thus the Federation of Communes will be born, governed by a Coordination Committee that will mark the line to be followed by all and impose it, by force, on those who are rebellious. Therefore, there will be another central power and, in the name of anarchy, the new anarchist State.

Communism, Marxist or Kropotkinian, of whatever kind or brand, can never achieve universal conformity and a world of identical puppets. But, to maintain itself, it will always have to be based on imposition and violence, on police forces and prisons.

Assuming, however, against all likelihood, that the economic conformity imposed by communism could become the reality of tomorrow, would it be able to make all friction and conflict disappear and fully realize universal harmony? Marxists believe so because, according to their simplistic materialistism, humans are equal sheep dominated only by the need for sustenance; and when everyone has a full stomach, they live in peace and always agree with each other.

I, on the other hand, believe the opposite, having a different conception of man. Even if it were possible to eliminate the economic causes that drive individuals against each other in armed conflict, war would still persist because there are other anthropological and psychological causes that determine conflicts. Today, I am forced to fight against my fellow human beings for a piece of bread and a woman. Tomorrow, communism will fill my stomach and the book of love will provide me with all the women I desire. But despite this, I will continue to fight to make my ideas triumph over others, either because I will envy my neighbor's strength or intelligence, or because I will be inspired by antipathy. The clash of passions and ideals generates hatred between men far more implacable than those that arise from the clash of interests. A feeling or faith, a thwarted inclination or a contested conviction, can drive people to fight better than the thirst for material pleasures.

It is vain to say that when the contradictions of economic interests are resolved and life is rationally organized, man will lose his antisocial impulses and spontaneously harmonize with his fellow human beings. Instead, man is not determined by interest and reason, as materialists and rationalists believe. He is an extreme, conflicted, and irrational being with different and opposing feelings, powerful and contradictory passions, and wants to satisfy them all. He wants to do good when he feels like doing good and evil when he feels like doing evil. Man demands freedom, but this is not the primacy of reason over the dark psychic background. Instead, it is the freedom of caprice, fantasy, instinct, romantic, individualistic freedom that rebels against the yoke of reason and mandatory well-being.

A great psychologist who has delved into the abyssal depths of the human spirit, Dostoevsky, wrote about this:

> There is one case, one only, when man may consciously, purposely, desire what is injurious to himself, what is stupid, very stupid—simply in order to have the right to desire for himself even what is very stupid and not to be bound by an obligation to desire only what is sensible. Of course, this very stupid thing, this caprice of ours, may be in reality, gentlemen, more advantageous for us than anything else on earth, especially in certain cases. And in particular it may be more advantageous than any advantage even when it does us obvious harm, and contradicts the soundest conclusions of our reason concerning our advantage—for in any circumstances it preserves for us what is most precious and most important—that is, our personality, our individuality. [13]

Life is not governed by rational or economic

13   Fyodor Dostoyevsky, translated by Constance Garnett, *Notes from Underground*, London: Heinemann, 1918.

laws, it is not regulated by staid starched formulas or cold deterministic theories, but rather

> it is an inexhaustible source of the unexpected and always new wealth, a tumultuous and fertile force that goes beyond human predictions and programs, to assert itself according to its secret rhythm.

Man is not all of one piece, not all logical or utilitarian, but is a problematic and mysterious being who reveals himself in continuously new ways by surrendering to the different and opposing passions that erupt from his dark depths. Reason will never be able to discipline these passions as it will never be able to subject life to its rules. Nietzsche said that "bad and antisocial passions, hatred, envy, greed, spirit of domination, exist deeply, essentially in life";[14] and Dostoevsky taught that "human nature is not reducible to the operations of reason. There will always be an irrational remainder that will be the source of life."

Therefore, social harmony is a vain chimera. The world will never establish that kingdom of "happy cowards" of which Leconte de Lisle speaks with

---

14   Martucci is paraphrasing here, condensing the quotation. The Italian translation was published as *Al Di Là Del Bene Del Male* Torino, 1898, but it is very close to the German, and the 1906 Englishing by Helen Zimmern: "If, however, a person should regard even the emotions of hatred, envy, covetousness, and imperiousness as life-conditioning emotions, as factors which must be present, fundamentally and essentially, in the general economy of life..."

contempt. Man needs struggle to fully develop his personality, to temper himself in danger, to dare and triumph. And the richer and more complex his soul is, the more he abandons himself to conflicting impulses and fights for both holy and evil causes, reveling in the arbitrary freedom of Dostoevsky's underground man or Nietzsche's *superman*.

Those who want to impose universal good and pretend to transform the world into an Eden are like the Grand Inquisitor in *The Brothers Karamazov*: fanatical tyrants who violate life, oppress humanity, and shed rivers of blood for the realization of an impossible dream.

The idea of universal brotherhood has had *auto-da-fés* and guillotines at its service: today it has the blow to the neck of the GPU.[15]

Stalin descends from Torquemada.

---

15   Today the Russian political police have changed their name. But it's still the same thing. [ENZO]

FACE TO FACE WITH THE SECT

During 30 years of revolutionary struggle, I often found myself with communists in Italy and abroad, in prison or in exile. Thus, I had the opportunity to get to know them thoroughly and to understand what a serious danger they represent for the future of humanity.

From the beginning, a reciprocal and violent antipathy manifested itself between us. Stalin's servants hated me, and I attacked them every time I had the opportunity. Our disagreement was not only determined by the diversity of ideas but also by the irreconcilable opposition of temperaments.

I have the restless and tormented soul of a romantic, a Dionysian soul, refractory to constraint and thirsty for distance. My excessive sensitivity, my ardent passions, the desperate longing for a new life and boundless freedom make me a brother of those poets, wanderers and nostalgics who, during the 19th century, sought the craziest intoxications beyond any stable order. With Nietzsche, I could unfurl the sails and dream of a warm tropical south or an indelible indigo-clad Greece; with Stirner, I could head towards a chaotic future and invoke a wild anarchy, licentious like a Bacchante with pert breasts and hair in the wind; with Baudelaire, I could aspire to the poisoned fragrance of the flowers of evil and go mad with desire for a beauty that descends from heaven or hell but makes the universe less sordid and time less heavy.

But with Gramsci or Togliatti, Roveda or Boretti, I could not get on a popular train and go to Moscow. No! My nature would rebel...

Communists are not men; they are not even animals; they are automatons, devoid of feelings, cold as ice and driven solely by the fanaticism that in them is not a passion or an intense faith, but something that burns internally and drives them to struggle and sacrifice, a *rational utilitarian duty*. "My reason," says the Bolshevik, "shows me that my interest as a proletarian is to become a communist. Therefore, I join the party, obediently obey the leaders, devote myself entirely to the cause, and even die in its service. But I do all this always for a material interest, to socialize wealth and create a new world in which I—if I survive—and all the other workers can eat and live well."

Naturally, the communist also has the unconfessed hope that in the future society they will be able to eat a little more than others and exercise authority as a people's commissar or agent of the GPU or, failing that, as a Soviet custodian of Vespasian monuments. Commanding, dictating law is a communist passion. Eating and commanding: these are the only two needs of the conscious Bolshevik. Apart from these, there are no others. And since communism promises the satisfaction of these two supreme demands, the Bolshevik fanatically fights for the advent of Stalin.

But this cold, materialistic fanaticism dictated by reason, which shows that it is better to suffer today in order to enjoy tomorrow, this fanaticism based on calculation and devoid of any outburst of feeling, of any warmth of ideal, of any breath of dream, is the most monstrous thing one can imagine. It is the only driving force of creatures with an arid soul and frozen blood, the only substitute for human passions that are lacking, by a whim of nature, or that have been suffocated by Marxist education.

Approach a follower of Stalin: live with him; you will be astonished by the absolute absence of any sensitivity, by the icy coldness of this red-enameled machine. Listen to his definitions—feeling: weakness, stuff for hysterical women. Pity: a faintness for a man with a full belly. Love: a lie; there is only sexual need; possessing a woman is like drinking a glass of water.[16] Art: a luxury for the bourgeoisie, a useless thing; it distracts from political struggle. Ideal: the ideological transposition of class interests. Will: an illusory appearance of economic determinism over which it exerts no action. Reality: the need of the belly.

Voltaire said that reading Rousseau's works made him feel the desire to walk on all fours. After talking to a communist, I feel the need for a feast of spaghetti.

16   Clara Zetkin "Lenin on the Women's Question" (1915): "You must be aware of the famous theory that in communist society the satisfaction of sexual desires, of love, will be as simple and unimportant as drinking a glass of water."

A Sicilian surveyor, V.G., whom I met in prison in Genoa in 1925 and met again in 1937 on the island of Tremiti, where he was politically exiled like me, was fond of poetry. When I asked him in front of his companions if he had written more verses, he blushed. He was ashamed to have spent his thoughts and time on lyricism that he should have devoted solely to the *idea*.

Professor Torelli (the one who confuses Kantism with Gentilean idealism) told me that a mechine operator is more useful to humanity than a poet. "Dante and Shakespeare are worth less than a skilled worker; poetry is useless," he said with a tone of superiority. However, I replied that only university professors who grant degrees to beasts like him are useless. We argued, and once, carried away by anger, he shouted, "Yes, we don't know what to do with poets. When communism comes, we'll make them unload coal in the ports."

The zealous Stalinist Domenica Montemartini, whom I found in Tremiti in 1935, enthusiastically reported to me that in Russia, women work like men, in factories, and also do the work of stokers, laborers, etc.

"That's not fair," I observed, "because a woman cannot bear heavy work. In front of a blast furnace, her skin burns, her flesh loses all softness and candor. If you force her to carry weights, her back curves. If you make her file or plane, her hands deform. A woman can only do those light tasks that do not make her lose her beauty."

Montemartini burst out laughing.

"We can do without beauty," she replied. "In communist society, there will be women with large, calloused hands and curved bodies, but production will increase."

It is in the name of this narrow utilitarianism that the Bolsheviks want to sacrifice everything else to the increase of material production. In their materialistic myopia, when a man's belly is full, he is satisfied and feels no other need. The demands of the intellect and feeling do not exist, life is reduced to a bowl of rice and a steak, happiness is in a full stomach. Even women, distorted by communist education, have lost the attributes of femininity, have masculinized themselves in the worst sense of the word, displaying brutality, roughness, rudeness, in contempt of the grace and refinement of their sex. They do not know love, deny the emotional bond, admit only the physiological function. When they give themselves, out of bestial lust, whoever possesses them has the sensation of mating with a bitch. Then, after the act, they leave the man without a kiss, without a caress, and go off with their comrades to talk about the five-year plan and Stalin's shrewdness.

One of these women who came to bed with me in a hotel in Naples took advantage of the opportunity to try to indoctrinate me. While I, exhausted from the long battle, rested my head on her breast and drank in the perfume of her young and fresh flesh, she, instead of talking to me about love, talked to me about communism.

Bored by the sermon which, at that moment,

was more than ever importunate, I asked her:

"You Communists assert that social harmony will be the inevitable product of history, that general and permanent agreement among men will be realized as a result of conditions which will inexorably come to pass. Well, why do you want to impose the dictatorship of your party violently and crush all those who do not think like you? Why do you instill in your comrades fanaticism, insensitivity, cruelty, in order to transform them into perfect sectarians, devoted solely to the cause and determined to make it triumph by any means? Let everything go its own way, do not fight, do not conspire, and what must happen, as a result of economic determinism, will happen."

"But we want to accelerate the historical process, hasten the disintegration of capitalist society," she replied promptly.

"But the historical process will not let itself be accelerated by you, and it will take all the time it wants. So if you stop telling me so much nonsense and kiss me on the mouth and tell me you love me, in the year 3100 Marxism will still be established in the world, thanks to the infallible laws that govern the course of human events."

The zealous Bolshevik got angry, jumped out of bed, dressed and left without saying a word to me. And I had to spend the night alone, giving blessings to Stalin and Karl Marx.

The Jew of Trier, in his essays on Feuerbach, sketched out a philosophy of praxis that is close to those other philosophies that have developed more fully since then and that tend to overcome the gnoseological dualism, the distinction between self and non-self. The subject poses the object which reacts on the subject that posed it.

The self represents the world, feels it, represents it; the world, Marx said, is not given but the product of the senses. However, all the representations and sensations of the self come from the world; I can't think, want, and feel except in the forms that the world determines, that is, I can't think, want, and feel anything other than what the world offers me and in the way it presents it to me. Therefore, it is not possible to establish where the subject ends and the object begins and vice versa. Matter, for Marx, is not like for the ancient materialists, matter in itself, independent of human sensation, but the matter that I create with my feelings, the sensible matter, relative to humans; but this matter reacts on me and determines me with the needs it gives me, with material, economic needs.

This philosophy is based on a premise that other philosophies, quite different from the Marxist one, also start from; but it is precisely such a premise that I deny. I have not stopped at the old Kantian positions, but I have never been able to overcome the dualism of subject and object. I do not know if things are placed by me, as idealists claim, or if things exist in themselves, outside of me, as realists assure. I do not know if sensation is a reaction to the stimulus that the objective world exercises on my senses, or if it is instead a state of consciousness that extends into spatial and quantitative representation, as Bergson asserts. But I do know, however, that I exist and that as I, as a subject, I distinguish myself from the things that I posit or that exist in themselves (outside of me) as noumenon, according to agnosticism, or as knowable reality, according to rationalistic gnosis.

I am a reality and the world is another; and I know that I and the world do not form one and the same thing because I can think and feel in myself differently from how the world determines. Mystics think and feel the infinite, they even want to annihilate themselves in it; yet the idea of the infinite cannot be inspired by the world of finite creatures and things. There are essential needs, rooted tendencies within me that cannot come from outside, they cannot be identified with the effect of external causes, because in the external world, the element that would stimulate them within the soul is missing. Then it is possible to establish where the subject ends and the object begins. Where something that is only mine, that finds no external correspondences, is united with what corresponds to the outside, there is the self. Instead, where a foreign world begins that influences me as I react to it, because there are affinities and oppositions between us but never identity, the object begins.

Then whether this object is placed by me (according to idealism) or exists in itself (according to realism), is a question that does not interest me and, in any case, cannot destroy the distinction between subject and object. Because if the object is placed by me, by my spirit (individual, according to solipsism,

ENZO MARTUCCI

universal, according to idealism), then this spirit representing the object projects itself into it. But it is not necessary that in the projection, there is the entire projecting spirit. The spirit may not project its ultimate essence, the essence of itself, precisely to maintain something that distinguishes and opposes it to the other part of itself, which it has estranged from itself, to represent it as an object.

Instead, if subject and object are distinct and existing realities in themselves, the consequence is that they can influence each other but *only to a certain point*, beyond which the subject remains a subject and the object remains an object. The essence of each remains as it is and does not undergo the influence of the opposite essence.

Therefore, in light of both idealist and realist philosophy, the ego is an undeniable fact that cannot be annulled in the world from which it distinguishes itself. It cannot be confused or identified with other egos, with other spirits, with whom it has many affinities but combined with its own essence, its own way of being, which distinguishes and separates it from all others.

This observation equally contradicts the dualism of Thomas Aquinas that is resolved in the adjustment of the intellect to things, as well as the idealist monism of Hegel and the materialist monism of Marx that reach the final identification between the interior and exterior. However, this same observation also drives a relativistic philosopher who does not recognize any reality beyond the phenomenal to consider pluralism the most acceptable among all metaphysical hypotheses.

When I explained these things to Dr. Z. (who must now be a big shot beyond the Iron Curtain), she would respond that I am (how embarrassing) an idealist, and that the ego is an illusion, the individual does not exist.

"Your Marx has said the same thing," I would reply. "The individual is an abstraction, reality is social being. But I would like to know how a society could exist if there were no individuals who, by associating, form it. The individual, instead, can exist even without society, returning to a wild state."

"But that's what you anarchists want," Dr. Z. would respond. "You want to return to the state of nature, you are followers of Rousseau. But how is it possible to go back today? Mechanization leads to collectivism, increasing industrial civilization tends towards ever greater organization in which the individual will be absorbed and disappear. In the future world, there will be no more romantic types, individuality, but rather cogs in the social mechanism."

Doctor Z. is a woman in her thirties, blonde, attractive, not entirely masculinized like other communists, and capable of winning a man's sympathy. She never came to bed with me, although she proposed it several times, and therefore I was left with the unsatisfied desire to lavish her with caresses.

But at that moment, instead of caresses, I would have given her a slap. How eagerly and with what immense pleasure the communists speak of the

ENZO MARTUCCI

annihilation of the individual...

They have only one goal: depersonalization. They want to smother the vivid colors of individuality in the uniform grayness of the undifferentiated mass. They dream of a humanity of automatons, perfectly alike, who move mechanically in the industrial barracks. They aspire to a life regulated and disciplined down to the smallest details, a life that is like a precision clock. They hate originality, freedom, unpredictability, and romance. And they praise organization and science so much because they believe that the scientificization of the world will produce the type they desire. The man without feelings and spontaneity, the automaton.

Nietzsche wrote that life must be given a heroic sense. The communists would like to give it a mechanical sense. But the growing mechanization, the exacerbated industrialism that depersonalizes man, are not fatal tendencies of civilization. They can be slowed down, and the individual can be prevented from being transformed into a machine's cog.

Romantic and individualistic, by temperament and conviction, I necessarily had to break with the communists, although like them, I fought against bourgeois society. Passionate and lyrical seeker of virgin forests and tropical intoxication, I could not confine myself to the industrial barracks with the fish-blooded and stick-eyed Bolsheviks.

Face to face with the sect, in Italy and abroad, in jail and in exile, I spat my contempt in their face.

MEMORIES OF THE '20S

In 1920, at the age of 16, I began to struggle against the bourgeois society and against the Bolsheviks, the odious representatives of the new order, totalitarian and demagogic, who were to inherit the dying capitalism.

At that time, I had run away from home, escaping from my father's discipline which weighed heavily on me, and I had reached Errico Malatesta in Milan, who had returned a few months earlier from London.

Born in Caserta into a bourgeois family, raised among people who went to church every Sunday and had the cult of institutions and social conservatism, I, a fifteen-year-old student, had become an anarchist through the philosophical and literary readings to which I passionately devoted myself and, above all, because of my rebellious temperament, intolerant of any restraint and any command.

When my relatives learned of my ideas and knew that I expressed them publicly, they were struck by the lightning of surprise and anger.

"How is it possible, Ninnillo, that you want to

become a petroleum dealer, you who were born a gentleman?" asked my good, old grandmother, anguished.

My father, a literature professor in state high schools, feared by students for his severity and the inflexible discipline he maintained in school, demanded that I renounce my ideas and inflicted the harshest punishments on me in the hope of bending me.

He achieved nothing but making me run away from home after five or six months of fierce arguments.

I first went to Salerno, where I was hosted by the socialist secretary of the Labor Chamber, Nicola Fiore; then I went to Milan to meet Errico Malatesta, for whom the Neapolitan dentist G.I. gave me a letter of introduction.

I agreed with the old anarchist agitator in the early days: I accompanied him on his propaganda tour of northern Italy and spoke together with him in speeches, impressing the crowds with my young age and the revolutionary enthusiasm that I poured into my speeches.

But then, driven by my temperament that pushed me further and further to the left, I became an individualist anarchist and sharply criticized the constitution of the Italian Anarchist Union, which was formed under the auspices of Malatesta and his two lieutenants Luigi Fabbri and Camillo Berneri. Although I was a young man, I was more logical than the big shots of official anarchism and understood that by organizing, libertarians would inevitably fall under discipline and the direction of leaders, and thus end up without government. I understood that the party suffocated anarchy and rebelled against this miserable degeneration that undermined the idea for which I had fled my family and interrupted my studies. Therefore, I broke with Malatesta and moved to Vigevano to be with the companions of that city who considered me a propagandist.

At that time, I still believed that the crowds, convinced by my words, could help me realize the great nihilistic dream, destroying all material and spiritual chains, all institutions and dogmas, and establishing unlimited freedom for all in the world. I did not cultivate the illusion of future social harmony, but believed that free struggle, tempered by spontaneous alliances and agreements, would be preferable to the unbearable yoke of laws and morals. I thought that in today's society, man, prostrated by obedience, does not defend himself against the tyrants who oppress him and becomes the victim of their abuses and harassments. But when everyone no longer wants to submit to others and tries to live independently, no one will be able to bend him. In an anarchist world, every individual, without God and without master, will increase his own strength by any means to use it when he cannot agree with his neighbors. The strong will remain so, but the weak, spurred on by necessity and freed from all ethical and legal restraint, will develop greater energy. Man may die in battle, but as long as he remains alive, he will be free. And if the social order breaks down, so much the better. For too long, we have vegetated in the flock: now life must be dangerous and intense. It is better to live one day as a lion than a hundred years as a sheep. Malatesta condemns Bonnot, but he is the true anarchist we should be inspired by.

Animated by ideas that were so different from those of my companions (?), I urged the slaves to overthrow the existing order. "But it's not enough to overthrow the current masters," I added, "we must prevent others from taking their place, and the socialist or communist dictatorship from being established. Man must become free, he must recognize neither bosses nor leaders. The greatest shame for an individual is to obey, because by obeying he shows that he cannot stand on his own two feet, that he is like a child who needs the protection and guidance of his father. But we want to do what we like, we want to understand or diverge as we please. You proletarians often shout, 'Bring on Lenin!' But don't you think that he too will be a tyrant who, under the pretext of maintaining order, will make you work under the lash?"

Naturally, these speeches did not please the socialist leaders, who professed to be disinterested and hypocritically declared that they aspired to power only for the good of the proletariat. But I rebuked them at every rally and loudly declared that they were swindlers who wanted to govern in order to fill their wallets and oppress the workers. And when they replied that I was promoting disorder, I retorted, "Yes, better disorder because it will not cause humanity as much damage as your dictatorship would."

In Vigevano, I had become the bane of demagogues. When I appeared at rallies and asked for the floor, the secretary of the Labor Chamber[17] got a fever. On June 6, 1920, at a public meeting called to protest against the increase in the price of bread, I spoke so violently that the public safety commissioner arrested me. The crowd, at my invitation to overthrow all authorities and snatch wealth from the bourgeoisie, attacked the police. The commissioner was beaten, the carabinieri were disarmed. Two socialist deputies, the secretary of the Labor Chamber and all the representatives of the P.U.S.[18] bravely took to their heels. I, a sixteen-year-old boy, took the lead of the riot.

I remained master of the city until evening. Then the royal guards arrived from Pavia and the reaction began. I miraculously escaped the search and fled to Milan. I continued to carry out my agitation, but I ended up convincing myself that the revolution would not break out.

The temperature had risen under high pressure, and the crowds longed for the wealth of the bourgeoisie as they descended into the squares with threatening intentions, but it was enough to increase wages, a trivial concession, to calm the boiling spirits and remove the danger. It was tavern revolutionary thinking back then. It erupted in invective against the government and the bigwigs, tumultuous in

---

17   Camere del Lavoro.
18   "Partito Unione Sindacale" (Trade Union Unity Party).

rallies, exhausted in strikes, but it never decided to take up arms and build barricades. The socialists who led the movement used the specter of insurrection to terrorize the bourgeoisie and blackmail Giolitti. They thus obtained everything they wanted, dominated in parliament and in the country, secured generous perks and lucrative jobs, and never even thought of making a real revolution. They preached it in the squares to scare the capitalists and force them to give in to the continuous demands; but then, when they saw the masses ready to act, they themselves slowed them down, saying that it was not yet the right time, calmed them down with the little gift of improved pay, and sent them to the taverns to sing "Quando Verrà Lenin" and shout, between one drink and another, "Lenin will come." The gullible proletarians appeared terrible when the red leaders posed as arsonists, but they immediately calmed down and gave up the '48 if any rascal from the P.U.S. climbed onto a table and said that they had to, yes, overthrow the bourgeoisie, but not immediately, rather tomorrow or later, when the leaders would give the signal. The racket continued, the workers yelled and went on strike, but they did not push any further, the frightened bourgeoisie regained courage, and all those demagogues, opportunists, and bread-seekers who had gathered around the socialist banner ate to their hearts' content and filled their wallets. Devoid of any idea and spurred only by insatiable hunger, they thought that it would be foolish to confront the royal guard and the lead of its muskets now that the trough was full and the government was compliant. The revolution had to serve for rally speeches, but to translate it into reality was quite another matter. Why spoil digestion and risk danger instead of being content with the assured grub and the medal won?

The Communists, still united with the Socialists, thundered against the leaders of the P.U.S. and accused them of betrayal; but essentially, they did nothing either and remained disciplined to the orders of their leaders.

The anarchists were few and could not, alone, drag the masses. Malatesta deluded himself with the hope of a united front and let himself be towed by the Socialists, bringing with him all the organized comrades, under his direction, in the Italian Anarchist Union.

The situation did not appear promising and I understood the revolution would not happen and that Socialists and Populists would continue to rule, luring the masses and blackmailing the bourgeoisie which, in the end, would have surrendered to the reaction. I realized that the power of demagogues and priests, of the D'Aragona and Don Sturzo, would be followed, in the short term, by a hangman's government that would have crushed any desire for subversion and restored order. And even if these dark predictions had not come true and the sudden revolution had overwhelmed the old world, what would have come of it? The anarchy I longed for? No, the dictatorship of Bombacci and Misiano, the Bolshevik despotism of which I would have been the first victim.

Despite this, I continued to fight and tried to inflame the masses and push them against everyone, against bourgeois society, socialism and communism, for the realization of the libertarian ideal. I became displeasing to God and to his enemies and while the royal guards shot at me in Milan, Malatesta attacked me in *Umanità Nova*[19] and, shortly thereafter, in Lomellina, the Socialists organized an attack against me which I escaped by pure chance. On July 29, 1920, in Voghera, I commemorated Gaetano Bresci in a public speech and was reported for apologizing for regicide. I spoke at two other rallies and other complaints rained down on me for incitement to crime and incitement to hatred between social classes. I was referred to the judgment of the Court of Assisi in Voghera and forced to flee to avoid arrest.

By now I was deeply disillusioned and understood that the masses would not only fail to establish anarchy but would not even make the revolution. After all, what would a tamed revolution have accomplished that would have sent away the king and the bourgeoisie to replace them with Turati and Don Sturzo, or even Bombacci and Misiano? What benefit would have come from replacing the fox of Dronero with Giacinto Menotti Serrati, the one who had been called spy No. 8 and accused of denouncing Luigi Galleani to the police in America?

The radical transformation of life, the great

---

19   *Umanità Nova* was an Italian anarchist newspaper founded in 1920. It was published daily until 1922 when it was shut down by the fascist regime.

metamorphosis I aspired to, could not be realized in reality because the crowds were gregarious, they could not exist without a shepherd, and they would not send him away except to put themselves under the tutelage of another. I should no longer hope for the social Muspell[20] from whose flames the heroic youth of the *unique one* would be born, but rather consider anarchy as the eternal revolt of the irreducible individual against all history's successive societies. I had to understand that the Promethean exception is destined to fight not only the states and the authorities but also the conservative instinct of the crowds lying in a millennium-old habit of laziness. I had to—in the extreme resolution of my tragic despair—accept this eternal struggle of the reprobate against everyone and become intoxicated with the nepenthe that drips from its bosom.

"Individualism," Maurizio Barrés said, "is the feeling of the impossibility of reconciling the particular self with the general self." And in the twilight of my last illusions, on the coffin of my dreams of universal regeneration, I fixed my open eyes on the fearful night of the battle without respite and prepared myself to plunge into the snare of its darkness to seek the distant stars and die.

Moved by these sentiments, I expressed them in some articles that were published in the magazine *L'Iconoclasta* of Pistoia. But throughout Italy, only one person agreed with me, a young self-taught, intelligent and rebellious man, Renzo Novatore, who,

---

20   Mythic Norse realm of fire.

ENZO MARTUCCI

two years later, fell under the bullets of the ferocious police. Instead, the miserable group of writers, semi-anarchists and Malatestians, attacked me and, from their newspapers, thundered their anathemas. Those pale libertarians who dreamed of the sugary quiet of an inevitable city of the sun, of which they aspired to become the conductors of general harmony, furiously attacked me and Novatore who advocated an individualistic and Promethean anarchism, a personal insurrection that dissolved every social organization, even hypocritically camouflaged with the anarchist mask. At the head of the group stood the philosophy professor Camillo Berneri, who possessed a truly black soul and tended towards the establishment of a libertarian church directed by his authority as a high priest.

Berneri, who wanted to replace one dogma with another, one religion with another, one organized and moralized society with another organized and moralized society, necessarily had to hate those, like me and Novatore, who wanted to destroy all dogmas, all religions, all ethical and social organizations, in order to make the natural freedom of the individual triumph, freed from all constraints and restored to spontaneity. Therefore, against me and Novatore, Berneri vomited all his bitterness. And he received the praises of the worshipping church for the new inquisitor who demanded the heads of the damned heretics.

Later, after Malatesta's death, Berneri became an even bigger piece of the anarchist group, and he fled to France where he had unclear relations with a fascist spy, a certain Menapace. Finally, in 1937, he was killed in Spain by Stalinist thugs, due to rivalry between the opposing churches.

Meanwhile in Italy, in that now distant autumn of 1920, I was living sad and unforgettable days. Forced to constantly flee, to move from one place to another to avoid arrest; subversively boycotted by my companions in Caino; without means and only having the poor help provided by some rare friend; I felt the circle tightening around me more and more, and I would not be able to escape the clutches of the police. Despite this, passing through Pistoia, I met Alfonsina Angioli and fell in love with her. She was a nineteen-year-old girl, with languid and sensual eyes that unleashed a storm in my veins, a hurricane I could not resist. I wanted her and she became mine. When I left, she demanded to follow me. She knew the desperate condition I was in, but despite this, she did not want to separate from me. And I, who loved her so much, did not have the strength to push her away. However, holding her close to my chest on a train seat speeding through the night, I thought with horror that at any moment, I could lose her. All it took was for a policeman to recognize me and it would all be over.

We hid in Naples and I found a way to make an agreement with a sailor who would have us embark on a ship headed to Marseille. But to hide on board, he wanted two thousand lire: and I didn't even have 2,000 cents. I turned to the old and emphatic leader of

ENZO MARTUCCI

the Neapolitan anarchists, but he replied that he did not have any money. Indeed, while Ciccio Cacozza was dying of hunger and I was about to end up in jail, he, the altruist, the libertarian from head to toe, left his apartment in via Duomo every evening with a trail of friends and went to carouse in a brewery in piazza Garibaldi. And he paid with the money sent to him by the anarchists in America to help political victims...

Cornered, after the refusal of my Neapolitan *comrades*, I was forced to turn to my mother. I asked her to send me the money without my father's knowledge. Alfonsina served as an intermediary because I couldn't go to Caserta, where I was so well known. But she was not known and could secretly meet with my mother without any danger.

Unfortunately, a *good* relative informed on my father. The professor handed the girl over to the police. At the police station, Alfonsina refused to speak and would not say where I was, so they sent her to jail. Meanwhile, in Naples, not seeing her return, I was in the grip of anguish, the most terrible agony, and I sensed what had happened.

The anarchist leader, the altruist from the brewery, introduced me to a one-eyed man, "a good communist comrade who sympathizes with anarchy." "He," said the leader, "is willing to go to Caserta and find out. If Alfonsina has been arrested, we will hire a lawyer to release her. She doesn't have to answer to anything, and they can't detain her. And you will get her back soon, and you will go to France together."

The leader's words lifted me a little, the one-eyed communist left for Caserta and returned in the evening with my father and the police who arrested me. My beloved father preferred to hand me over to the police rather than leave me outside "to be an anarchist," as he said with contempt. He knew very well that I had to answer to the Court of Assisi for my revolutionary activity, but for his bourgeois conscience, it was better that I was arrested because *"the scandal would end, and the family's decorum would not receive any more insults."*

The one-eyed communist, as a reward, received ten lire from my father. And he drank it in the evening, at the inn, cheering for Lenin, with his comrades.

I was supposed to be confined to a juvenile detention center awaiting trial, but since my family had already requested my internment in a correctional facility, I was sent to the "Ferrante Aporti" reformatory in Turin.

There, shortly after, the director, believing that I could spread my ideas among the others, isolated me in a punishment cell. And I stayed there for six months.

At seventeen years old, buried alive in that tomb where there was no air or light except for what filtered through the wolf-mouth window, defended by a sturdy iron grate, I, so sensitive and already shaken by so many emotions, felt like I was going crazy. The anguish suffocated me, and I could only take five steps forward and five steps back: from the door to the wall and from the wall to the door. I never saw anyone except for the guard who brought me soup; even outside, in the courtyard, they only sent me there during the regular hour. They didn't give me books, didn't allow me to smoke, and treated me with the utmost severity. Winter had come, and there was no heating in the cell, and I was literally freezing. In the morning, at six o'clock, they forced me to get up, folded the cot against the wall and secured it with a lock, preventing me from lying down during the day and seeking a little warmth among the blankets. In that horrible hole, so narrow and sad, devoid of any distraction that would direct my thoughts elsewhere and plagued by nostalgia and memories, I suffered terribly with the fixed idea of Alfonsina. I understood that I would never see her again because I would leave the reformatory only to go to prison after the trials and conviction, and stay there for several years. I imagined that she would end up in another man's arms, and jealousy gnawed at me. I remembered her kisses, her caresses, her tender abandonments, and felt a powerful need for them; then, thinking that I would never enjoy them again, I plunged into a dark, mortal melancholy that physically and morally prostrated me.

"For me, she ruined herself," I kept saying, "she left her family, who will never accept her back. And now that I'm here, how will she survive? Will she be forced to prostitute herself and end up insane in a hospital? And will the police continue, out of hatred for me, to persecute her? And what end, what abyss, what torment will be reserved for her?"

The agony drove me mad, and the nervous crises and desperate outbursts that sometimes led me to hit my head against the wall in the hope of breaking it were followed by dark depressions in which I remained annihilated, humiliated, abandoned to the pain that tore me apart with the skilled perfidy of an experienced executioner.

In that horrible cell where Giovanni Giolitti's liberal Italy had relegated me, the first silver threads appeared in my hair. And I was only seventeen years old!

Meanwhile, in a beer hall in Naples, the anarchist leader and the communist spy were drinking glasses to the health of the revolution. And they were paying with the money from the Committee for Political Victims, the same money that should have been used to help me escape abroad.

ENZO MARTUCCI

FROM THE EXILES

I stayed in the reformatory for a year, spending six months in the horrible cell I will never forget and six, sick, in an infirmary cubicle. Then I got out because, for political processes, I obtained provisional freedom and my father, pressured by my grandparents and his wife, asked the President of the Court to return me to him, even though recognized as irredeemable by the family and the law.

Accompanied by the professor who catechized me from Turin to Caserta, I returned to this city and spent two years under the domestic roof to which I had not returned with the repentance of the prodigal son. But finally, tired of political persecutions and quarrels with my dad, obtusely tyrannical, I moved to Venice. After a few months, I learned that the discussion of my processes had been scheduled at the Court of Assizes in Voghera and, to escape the effects of the sentence, I took off and reached France after many adventures.

When I arrived on the soil of the republic, my soul was still intoxicated by the harsh beauty of the Alps and the proud solitude of the peaks that I had overcome with the guidance of a smuggler. However,

I only had a small bouquet of edelweiss picked in the snow at about three thousand meters high in my pocket. The few one-hundred notes I possessed had gone for travel expenses and guide payment, and I did not know how to reach Paris without means.

In Grenoble, I found an Italian worker, a good man, who accompanied me to the communist club. When I entered, there was a meeting, and in front of the crowded room, a Piedmontese spoke, the head of the Bolshevik exiles in Isère. He argued for the need to unite against the fascist danger and to form a revolutionary united front to overthrow Mussolini.

"All workers," he said, "whether socialists or communists, syndicalists or anarchists, must unite in a single bundle and forget the ideological divergences that separate them. They must understand each other with a fraternal spirit, help each other and fight alongside each other to overcome the bourgeois reaction that rages in Italy."

The audience greeted these words with thunderous applause, and the orator continued his speech, dragging himself into the usual commonplaces of Bolshevik phraseology. I had not eaten since the day before, and I did not know where I would spend the night; my head was spinning tried to demonstrate to those I spoke with about it the absurdity and ferocity of the action organized against a potentially innocent person. Finally, the leader stopped, they talked to him about me, and he wanted to meet me.

"Are you an anarchist comrade fleeing from Italy?" he asked me. "Do you have pending processes? Well,

well, but here you are safe. However, there are no an-archists in Grenoble. At least, I do not know any. It means that if you stay here, you will be with us. Today, we must unite as brothers against the fascist enemy."

Other communists approached and spoke to me. While I was talking to them, the worker who had accompanied me called the leader aside and, on his initiative, before I could stop him, asked for help for me. "He is a political victim who has no money to go to Paris. Let us give him some," he said.

"But are you crazy?" replied the other. "He is an anarchist, our enemy. And you want us to help him?"

"But you yourself just said that we must unite with anarchists and socialists to fight fascists," the worker replied.

"Yes, I said it because it is necessary for them to come with us, against fascism. But then we will immediately scam them. Do you know what Lenin said? 'We must use the anarchists during the revo-lution and shoot them immediately after.' However, if we can give them a little tap on the back without them noticing, that's a gain. This is Marxist politics, my dear."

The two spoke in a low voice so as not to be heard by me, but I, with good hearing, listened to everything. The worker who did not agree with the boss's duplicity came back to the attack.

"I don't think it's right to leave him like this, in the middle of the street. He has nothing to eat and nowhere to sleep. What do you expect him to do?"

"Let him figure it out," replied the other. "I'm

happy that he's in trouble. This way, he will realize that discipline is necessary in the revolutionary struggle."

At this point, unable to hold back any longer, I approached the two and, addressing the boss, said:

"I knew for a long time that you Communists are sectarian and hypocritical. But I am pleased to once again note your immense cowardice. You call us for help with a sweet smile, while keeping a knife ready under your jacket to strike us. However, you will not do to us here what you did in Russia. Here we will break your horns. Know, for your information, my little Lenin, that even if you had offered me the help that your friend asked for on his own initiative, I would not have accepted it. But you, who are happy about the difficulties of a rebel who fled from Italy with three court cases hanging over his head, you are not a revolutionary but a scoundrel."

I turned my back and left. I spent the night in a building under construction, sitting on a stone. The next day, I managed to get a job as a laborer with the master builder of the masons and was able to eat. Then I met an Emilian anarchist who let me stay in his attic. After about two weeks, I left Grenoble and moved to Lyon.

I arrived in Paris in early October. I found many anarchists whom I had known in Italy, and they introduced me to the French comrades. At the *Le Libertaire*[21] editorial office, I met with the old Faure

_____

21   *Le Libertaire* was a Francophone anarchist newspaper established in New York City in June 1858 by the exiled

and with André Colomer who was then running the newspaper. I frequented the circles of exiles and in a café in Place du Combat, I had the good fortune to meet Stefano Kolnar, who had been a big shot in Hungary during the time of Bela Kun.

I collaborated with the Italian libertarian newspaper *La Rivendicazione*[22] which was published in the French capital. However, my individualist ideas soon put me at odds with the communist anarchists, led by Vezzana, Mosca, and Erasmo Abate, who had formed a Malatestaist and dogmatic church in the "Maison Comune" on rue de Bretagne.

Because I had dared to argue with Malatesta in the columns of *Umanità Nova*, defending individualism against communism, I was the black sheep of those sectarian fanatics. When Armando Borghi arrived a few days later with the small, yellow D'Andrea and presented himself at the editorial office of *Le Libertaire*, escorted by the knight in cloak and sword Meschi, we greeted each other briefly.

---

anarchist Joseph Déjacque. It appeared at slightly irregular intervals until February 1861. The title reappeared in Algiers in 1892 and was then produced in Brussels between 1893 and 1894. In 1895, *Le Libertaire* was relaunched as a weekly publication in France by Sébastien Faure and in the socially and politically turbulent years that accompanied rapid economic change during the run up to 1914 it became a leading title in a growing field of anarchist newspapers and journals. Publication persisted from 1918 until 1939 and then from 1944 until 1956.

22   *La Vindicazione* was a historic Italian anarchist magazine, published in Forlì, the capital of Romagna at the end of the 19th century. In the 1920s an Italian-language magazine with the identical title was founded in Paris.

Every Sunday, at the "Maison Comune," I argued with the faithful of Saint Errico, to whom I repeated in every possible tone that their Anarchist Union was absurd and ridiculous and that libertarian communism constituted a mistaken compromise between Bolshevik authoritarianism and Stirnerian individualism.

One day, the *Errico-ites* tracked me down to assault me, and Pietro Bruzzi, who was later executed by the Nazis, received a punch from Mosca because he agreed with me.

Furthermore, I criticized Malatesta for his not very sympathetic attitude towards the Diana bombers. In fact, he was arrested a few months after me as the instigator of the revolution. In Italy, fascist reaction had already violently erupted, made possible by the cowardice of the socialists who had not been able to barricade themselves; and this reaction, aided and financed by the bourgeoisie and its State, had felt the need to immediately remove the only revolutionary of a certain seriousness in the peninsula from circulation. Malatesta, imprisoned for several months, had begun a hunger strike at S. Vittore to protest against the judiciary, which never decided to set the date of his trial. But the judiciary did not give in, and Malatesta, after several days of fasting, exhausted by weakness, was about to die.

No one stood up for him. The proletariat, the eternal sheep, horned and bleating, who had briefly taken on the lion's mane but then, humiliated by the indecision and cowardice of its leaders and terrified

ENZO MARTUCCI

by fascist beatings, had returned humble and servile as before, did not stir from its inertia and allowed the old agitator to die of hunger in prison.

The socialists who had split from the communists thought of nothing else but to taunt each other. Gramsci, from the columns of *L'Ordine Nuovo*, hurled every qualifying adjective he could find in the brothel dictionary against Nenni, and Nenni (currently a staunch supporter of the communists) responded to Gramsci and the Bolsheviks from the pages of *L'Avanti*, using the same epithets that bitches use in their fiercest fights. So amidst the accusations they hurled at each other, the internecine struggle that tore them apart, and the reaction that weakened them, they didn't even think for a moment to lift a finger in defense of Malatesta. Besides, it wouldn't have bothered them if a state denier disappeared from this earth.

The organized anarchists made a lot of noise but nothing concrete. Gigi Damiani, from the pages of *Umanità Nova*, urged others to take action, declaring that if no one had moved to defend the old man, he would break his pen in protest. But no one moved, and Damiani didn't break his pen precisely because it served him then, as it serves him today, to maintain a salary as an anarchist journalist.

The only ones who intervened in favor of Malatesta were the individualists. Those individualists whom he had always fought and mocked. And they acted not only to defend a poor old man abandoned by all after a lifetime of revolutionary struggle, but also because they believed they could strike both the weak resignation of the crowds who tolerated the martyrdom of their apostle, and the vile ferocity of the ruling class who wanted to maintain its power with violence.

Boldrini, Aguggini, and Mariani detonated a bomb in Milan's Diana theater, causing deaths and injuries. Public opinion was outraged against the anarchists. Upon hearing the news, Malatesta condemned the attack and, as a protest against it, ended his hunger strike.

By doing so, he saved himself. Otherwise, he would not have been able to resume eating without being ridiculed and damaging his reputation as a hero who would rather die than give in. He always condemned the Diana attack, committed by "desperados who are not anarchists because anarchists believe in the future." He appeared before the Milan Court of Assizes as a utopian fleeing from terror and was acquitted.

But Mariani, Boldrini, and Aguggini, who acted in his defense, were sentenced to life imprisonment. They were condemned even more severely because, in public, everyone said their act was so infamous it aroused Malatesta's disapproval. Boldrini and Aguggini died in prison, and poor Mariani emerged after 25 years, exhausted and broken, falling into the hands of the followers of Saint Errico, who forced him to renounce his gesture.

I frankly expressed my unfavorable opinions about Malatesta's attitude towards the terrorists during the meetings of the "Maison Comune," drawing protests and the wrath of idiotic idolaters against me. They said that Errico had always been consistent because he had always condemned individual revolt. And I replied that, in the case of Diana, it had been more than useful to denounce terrorism. We argued fiercely and, many times, came to blows.

Finally, however, another event occurred that exacerbated my disagreement with the exiles of all stripes.

A man had been killed because he was suspected of being a spy or having worked as one. The so-called "avengers" wanted to inflict the same treatment on his lover. True, they had no evidence, nor even a remote hint, that she had cooperated in the dead man's shady activities. But she was his friend, and that was enough. Just for that reason she had to be a spy too. And they had to give her a "party" too.

In a dingy café in Place du Combat, I tried to demonstrate to those I spoke with about it the absurdity and ferocity of the action organized against a potentially innocent person. But all my arguments were not enough to overcome the stubborn obtuseness of two Bolshevik whitewashers and a Malatestian thug. In the end, in a burst of indignation that I could not repress, I declared the murder they wanted to commit was disgusting to me, and that I would try to prevent it even at the risk of my life. The thug gave me a fierce look. Then his lips twisted into a grin and, in an ironic tone, he said to me:

"Indeed, you want to play the knight... How ridiculous you are! You act like Don Quixote. But if you really care, I'll give you an opportunity to satisfy your Don Quixotism. The comrades have discovered that the female hangs out in a café in Place de la Nation. And they will go there to catch her and give her the lesson she deserves. You, who are such a knight, go to that café and protect her. You'll easily recognize her: she's a dark-haired, pale woman, dressed in blue, and her name is Irene. Stand by her side and you'll feel what it's like to be beaten."

"Tonight, I'll go there, no doubt. And send me the best chasers so they can make a fool of themselves like Misiano in Germany.[23] So, see you tonight."

I got the address of the café, procured a good pistol, and arrived on time. I found her in a corner, sitting next to a table on which a crumpled newspaper testified to the nervousness of the hands that had just left it. Under the geometric brim of the hat that covered almost all of her forehead, her black eyes had a mysterious something. They shone. Against the pallor of her face, her red lips stood out, infusing a sensual desire, a need to kiss and bite them.

---

23   Francesco Misiano (1884–1936) was an Italian Communist militant and politician who took part in the January Uprising in Berlin in 1919, and was sentenced to a decade in prison. He was let out due to political pressures and back in Italy he founded the Italian Communist Party (PCI). He would later move to Russia to play a significant role in Soviet cinema and the Communist Party. After a lifetime of faith to the cause, the Party turned against him.

ENZO MARTUCCI

Outside, beyond the windows, the fog thickened, enveloping the square in its increasing opacity. She watched the door as if waiting for someone and occasionally huddled in her dark coat with a cold gesture. She could be twenty years old, or at most twenty-two, but her pose betrayed a woman of life, a seller of love, troubled and uneasy for lack of clients.

And it was this poor girl that the exiles wanted to attack. She was the spy, the reprobate...

"Are you Irene?" I asked.

"Yes, do you know me?" she turned with the eagerness that a probable invitation inspired in her.

"Would you like something to drink?"

"Thank you, a coffee."

After a little while, I knew everything about her. The dead man was her lover, they had lived together for two months. He supported her, didn't make her walk the street again, which she had returned to out of poverty after the drama of Faubourg Saint Antoine. She didn't understand politics at all: she didn't profess fascism or communism, nothing. She only felt the weariness of life that she had to take up again and regretted the peace of the lost apartment.

"And aren't you afraid that those who killed your friend might do something to you?"

"To me? Why? I am a woman, I am not involved in their affairs. Besides, I am French, from Cannes. I have nothing to do with Italian issues."

"But you tried to defend your friend when they attacked him."

"Me? I saw those four who approached my table,

threatening him. I tried to calm them down. Then they attacked him, and I was afraid, very afraid. I ran away."

Remembering the tragic scene, she became even paler.

There were only a few customers left in the café. A waiter, leaning against the window, counted the tips he had earned in his pocket. Outside, the fog merged with the evening, and in the middle of the square, the statue of the Triumph of the Republic, in the crocodile pond, looked like a blurred point.

The door opened. Three individuals entered. I instinctively felt the danger. I didn't know them, but their Italian type didn't escape me. One of them, especially, had a grim face that I still remember. They sat at the table next to ours and stared at us fixedly.

The waiter had gone. In the semi-deserted café, only four or five people could be seen, all far from us. The newcomers seemed pleased with the favorable situation.

"Irene," one of them called.

"Don't answer," I said to her quietly. Then I continued in Italian:

"Look, Irene, at the purchase I made today. Do you like this trinket? I have the idea that someone will try it tonight."

I pulled the gun out of my pocket and put it on the table.

"But..." the frightened girl said.

"Shut up," I interrupted her abruptly. "Come with me."

I put the gun back in my pocket, staring into the eyes of the three men who didn't miss any of my movements. Then, taking the woman's arm, I led her out. None of the three moved. None dared to follow us.

In a distant restaurant, where I offered her dinner, I informed her of the danger. I advised her not to frequent places where she was known and to disappear. Then I gave her the few francs I had left, after paying the bill. I didn't want her to have a bad evening.

When she gratefully and surprisedly asked me if I would accompany her to the hotel:

"No, I can't," I replied. "I'm expected. I have to leave you."

I desired her so much. But I didn't mean to be paid for protection.

FIRST EXILE

1924-1933: nine years of struggle, tension, and agony. They mark the stormiest period of my life, the acute phase of the war of the outcast against everyone.

Returning to Italy following an amnesty, I could no longer leave it. In 1925, I was in prison in Genoa, and in 1933, after five years of political probation, I found myself in exile in Lampedusa. Rosa, the affectionate companion who had shared misery, persecution, and torment with me for seven years, had died, consumed by that hellish life. My family had disowned me, my mother paid for her financial ruin and the abandonment of her husband with her love for her son. A considerable inheritance I had received from an old aunt had disappeared in a few months. Lampedusa welcomed, in its oppressive desolation, the tragic wreck of a high-seas ship. All the stars had vanished, leaving only dark shadows and the sneer of fate.

As a prisoner on a sad island, thrown among the riffraff in the filth of the cells, I suffered the most atrocious tortures for the insane daring of revolt, the unheard-of desire to transform life, to adapt the world to me, to my Promethean dreams, to my romantic desires. And I remembered, with bitterness, the last blows I received, the attacks of the *squadristi*, the political persecution that had preceded my exile, and the infamous frames concocted against me by a perfidious police officer, the vice-questore of Caserta, who distinguished himself in spewing slanders and concocting trials against the outcast. Meanwhile, new pains added to the old ones, and I writhed in the chains that entered my flesh, feeling the overwhelming need to break free and throw myself back into the struggle, striking everything and everyone.

An attempt to escape from the island failed. A fisherman who was supposed to take me to Tunisia with his boat robbed me of my money and then reported me. I was immediately transferred to Tremiti, and on the arid cliff that drops steeply onto the waves of the Adriatic, I found only human refuse, political or common exiles, devoid of personality, sensitivity, and ideals.

Nauseated by the environment to which I could not adapt, exasperated by the restrictions imposed by my confinement, I decided to renew my attempt to escape from Lampedusa and, to this end, I made arrangements with Giuseppe Boretti. A bright young man, born like me into a bourgeois family and possessing a not insignificant culture, Boretti was the only one with whom I could exchange a few words in that horrible place. However, his Marxist fanaticism, his extreme sectarianism, made him unpleasant and often led our discussions to degenerate into bitter arguments.

Educated in a Jesuit college, then converted to communism, this son or grandson of a general had his soul desiccated by the precepts of Loyola and Marx and, with his lack of any feeling or humanity, with his passive obedience to the fixed idea that dominated him, increased my aversion to those two rigid disciplines that denature man and transform him into a blind instrument in the service of Catholicism or Bolshevism.

At twenty-two years old, he knew nothing of love: he did not feel the need for a woman. He did not conceive of friendship and confessed this frankly. One day he told me that in Milan, a few years earlier, while he and Amendola were getting out of a car, they were surrounded by a group of policemen who wanted to arrest them. Amendola threw himself against the policemen and engaged in a struggle. Instead, he, the scion of a general, ran away and saved himself by fleeing.

"But it was cowardice on your part," I observed to him, "you abandoned a friend in danger, you left him alone to deal with many. You should have stayed by his side, fought and fallen or saved yourself with your comrade."

"How presumptuous you are," he replied, with a smile of superiority. "By staying, I would have gone to jail and could not have served the party for a long time. By fleeing, I preserved my freedom and the possibility of continuing to be useful to communism. What do I care about friends? And what are they? The essential thing for me is the party."

Another time he told me that if I had ended up in Russia with him, he would have immediately denounced me and had me arrested.

"And would you have the courage to do that?" I replied. "We were in confinement together, we shared the same pain. Now we are trying to escape from here, facing risks and adversity that we must face together. And you, afterwards, would you hand over to the red police someone who fought and suffered with you?'"

"Yes, I would," he replied decisively. "You are not an anarchist like Failla, a halfway anarchist with whom we communists can come to an understanding. You are a true anarchist, an enemy of communism, and we must annihilate you. Don't you know that, to serve my idea, I would have my own mother shot?"

Sometimes, while sipping coffee at Angelina's bar, I looked at that young man sitting opposite me on the other side of the table, and it seemed to me that I was facing the bench of a Bolshevik tribunal, a red Fouquier-Tinville who was about to condemn me to execution. His face was too severe for his young age: behind the thin-framed glasses, the dark flame of fanaticism burned in a ruthless gaze. The gaze of an Inquisition Dominican, a heretic exterminator or even a Jacobin of terror or a prosecutor general in Stalin's synods.

Boretti defined me as a *decadent romantic* and, on other occasions, also "a depraved playboy who used the revolutionary platform to get into bed with the female workers of Cassano d'Adda".

I called him a *red priest* and advised him to rest in the beds of the GPU agents who, with the methods of Sodom, would inject him with new Bolshevik ardor.

We *often* insulted each other, and the irreducible opposition of ideas and temperaments created a deep abyss between us. However, we needed each other. I had found someone who, for financial compensation, would provide us with the boat with which we would escape to Dalmatia. He did not have the means to leave the island but could provide the five thousand lire that had been requested by the fisherman with whom I was negotiating. The plan failed because the money, which was supposed to arrive clandestinely, did not arrive. Shortly thereafter, Boretti was called to arms and, from the island of Elba where he had been sent, managed to cross over to Corsica. I remained in Tremiti and suffered the most severe restrictions from the management, who had sensed something about the escape plan.

Three or four months passed, and the attempt that I had failed to execute due to lack of money was instead attempted by two other political prisoners. One, a certain S., called "the Englishman" because he had spent his youth in England, was in Tremiti on suspicion of spying for the British government. He inspired me with a violent antipathy for his hypocritical and honeyed character and also for the qualities attributed to him as a spy.

As a staunch conservative, as only one who has

been educated in London schools can be, he fraternized with communists nonetheless, hoping to use them when the time was right. The truculent followers of Stalin, the unruly revolutionaries, polished the shoes of that caricature of a lord who, in his starched respectability and according to the rules of English liberalism, deigned to honor them with a smile that expressed the benevolence of a generous master to his zealous servants. And the heralds of universal subversion bent over backwards to buy pastries and jam from the baronet of Albion who, in his exquisite munificence, gave postage stamps to one lackey for his collection, coins for tobacco to another, and a non-working watch to a third.

Having a few hundred pound notes and overcoming the formidable fear that agitated his not very leonine heart, the illustrious representative of HIS MAJESTY attempted to flee, spurred on by the allure of luxurious restaurants that, on the banks of the Thames, offer every comfort and well-being to those who pay with money, even if it belongs to the Intelligence Service.

Cesare Neri joined his escape attempt, having arrived on the island of Tremiti just a few days earlier and not knowing what kind of ethical specimen the five-meal turkey was. He participated in the venture driven by his adventurous spirit and love of danger.

Neri was a different type from the Englishman. Passionate and impulsive, rebellious and rough, like a pure-blooded Romagnolo, always ready to ignite like a match but sincere and loyal, he immediately won my sympathy. On the day he arrived in the prison, as soon as he entered the barracks, he declared to everyone present:

"Guys, I am a fascist and convinced of my ideas. I am telling you this right away so that you know who you're dealing with. If you want to approach me and respect my opinions, as I will respect yours, all the better. Otherwise, everyone will go their own way without bothering the others."

Enthusiastic about his faith but free from sectarianism like myself, he approached me even though I had openly declared myself an anarchist. I preferred the company of Neri, a fascist, to that of the communists; Neri would approach me and keep three or four other convicts who claimed to be fascists and acted as informants for the authorities at a distance.

Not knowing English, the man from Romagna accepted the Englishman's proposal and attempted to escape with him. The fisherman who was supposed to take them away sold them out to the police. As they were leaving the island in a boat, another boat loaded with police emerged from a cove where they had been hiding and blocked the fugitives' path. Some shots were fired, and the Englishman, trembling like a leaf, threw himself face down in the bottom of the boat, while Neri, standing up, shouted at the agents, "Shoot these bastards, you sons of bitches."

Arrested and taken to the Manfredonia prison, they were sentenced to three months in prison. When they returned to the island, they were irreconcilable enemies: they had quarrelled in prison and S.

harboured a deep-seated hatred for Neri.

Meanwhile, the lawyer Giacomo Costa arrived, a Freemason, socialist sympathizer, former deputy of Naples, a great purveyor of empty promises, hypocritical and opportunistic, diplomatic and posturing like that crazy parliamentarianism that represents so well. Soon our relationship became tense because I couldn't stand his airs and all the nonsense he spouted to give himself importance, and I always argued back.

One day, in the tavern where we were having lunch, to make those present feel that he had met Lenin, he said to me:

"Anarchy is unrealizable. Lenin confirmed it to me too."

"According to him. But where did he tell you that?"

"In Switzerland."

"When?"

"In 1925 on the occasion of our last meeting."

"*To the soul of the lie!* Lenin left Switzerland in '17 and never moved from Russia until his death in '23 or '24."

"But if I tell you that in '25 I saw him in Lausanne..."

"Yes, the Almighty had given him permission to come and talk to you."

Another time, in the same tavern, he started:

"When I was Minister of Finance in Fiume, during the D'Annunzian occupation, I drafted the Statute of the Regency of Carnaro which D'Annunzio then approved."

"Indeed," I observed, "you dictated and Alceste De Ambris wrote. But when will you stop boasting?"

Costa could see me as smoke in his eyes, but he courted Neri because he knew that he was a friend of Arpinati. At the same time, he flattered S. thinking that even the Intelligence Service is a power and therefore, it is necessary to win the favor of its agents.

One morning, in the small square of the Castle where the management offices are located, only Neri, Costa, and I were walking around. Costa was telling us that he had refused the position of Minister of the Interior in the Bonomi cabinet and the presidency of the Council when Facta resigned. Neri was listening, and I was looking, with a covetous eye, at the Juno-like figure of beautiful Assuntina, the young laundress who was washing laundry outside her home.

"A few months ago," Costa said, "I sent the Duce an extremely important document that came into my possession thanks to the influential connections I have in international political circles. This document shows that the Greek Politis was in the service of the Negus. Mussolini, acknowledging receipt of it, wrote to me: 'Dear Costa, I thank you for the great service you have rendered to the country.'"

Assuntina had retreated into her hut, hiding from my gaze the alluring roundness of her voluptuous bosom. Annoyed, I vented my frustration on Costa:

"Mussolini responded differently to you. He wrote to you, 'Dear Costa, you talk nonsense, and to punish you, I will send you into exile.'"

The honorable *panzerotto*,[24] as I affectionately called him in the Neapolitan dialect, assumed an indignant air.

"One cannot have a serious conversation with you. You are so insolent...."

He didn't finish the sentence because a common prisoner who, after spending ten years in Portolongone, had become the personal secretary of the director of the colony in Tremiti, approached Neri.

"You speak ill of me," he shouted, "but know that I will make you feel my punches."

Talking about punches to Neri was like inviting him to bed with a beautiful girl. The ex-convict from Portolongone had not even finished his threat when a formidable direct hit landed on his face and sent him crashing into the wall. Bleeding and bruised, he didn't even attempt to retaliate and went to the infirmary to receive medical attention. A few minutes later, the police arrived and arrested Neri. Left alone, I found out and uncovered the plot against the Romagnolo. The Englishman had encouraged F. to provoke Neri, knowing that he, with his impulsive nature, would lash out and end up in jail. Immediately after the incident, two communists who were not present during the argument but who the deceitful Englishman had induced to give false testimony for a bribe of 20 lire, declared to the public safety brigadier:

---

24   The name of a savory turnover, resembling a miniature calzone.

"We were in the square when F. passed by. He didn't say anything to Neri, didn't provoke him in any way. Instead, the fascist jumped on him as soon as he saw him and beat him."

Costa, questioned in turn, got away with his usual diplomacy. He did not accuse Neri but did not displease S. He gave an ambiguous statement that ultimately harmed the arrested man.

The only one who had the courage to tell the truth to the colony director was me. I confirmed to him that the communists had not been present and had given false testimony. And when I realized that he did not want to believe my words, I shouted:

"You are persecuting Neri because, in Rome, he slapped Starace. That's why you blindly accept the lies of your enemies. But remember that I will repeat what I have told you to the prosecutor."

The Intelligence Service man, to get rid of his adversary, took advantage of F.'s indulgence, the malicious grudge that the colony director held against Neri, and the sectarian venality and hatred of the communists. The frame-up sent the Romagnolo to jail, but I explained the facts to the magistrate of Manfredonia, produced evidence of my statements, and Neri was acquitted after a month.

In Angelina's café, I spat in the face of an Englishman to show my contempt. He didn't dare react and, with a chicken-like twist of his neck, he swallowed all the insults I hurled at him. After some time, he sought revenge by plotting another underhanded scheme against me, which fortunately I foiled.

With the communists, I used no better words than those I had used with S. "You say you don't recognize bourgeois law and the state, yet you offer yourselves as false witnesses to this law to send a man to prison. Doesn't that seem like inconsistency, as well as cowardice?"

"Not at all," they replied, "because Neri is a fascist, and when it comes to striking a political opponent, we also use bourgeois law and spy on them. This is Machiavellianism."

I had to walk away because the urge to vomit was choking me. I am a disciple of Stirner and Nietzsche, a convinced amoralist, and I believe with La Rochefoucauld that evil, like good, has its own heroes. I understand Alexander the Great who conquers the East and dies from excess in Babylon, Nero who sets fire to Rome to satisfy an artistic fantasy, Napoleon who bathes Europe in blood dreaming of world domination, Bonnot who robs banks and heroically falls at Choisy le Roi, fighting alone against five hundred policemen. I understand the tyrant as well as the rebel, the ego that asserts itself in freedom, but I despise the slave as well as the spy, the ego that humbles itself, that crawls. I admit the evil that makes one great, even when it is not fortunate, the evil that translates the promethean effort, the strenuous struggle against the world; but I detest the abjection that reduces man to a worm-like creature and bends him to accept the existing order of things, exploiting its most sordid sides. Barabbas doesn't disgust me, but Judas does. And this is, for me, a matter of sentiment, not of morality.

The communists, on the other hand, prefer the other kind of evil, the cowardly and degrading one. After a few days of sending Neri to jail, they denounced an old republican, a certain Ragazzini, who had let slip some offensive words about the king. As a result of the denunciation, the old man got three and a half years in prison. And Stalin's followers got rid of a hated opponent whom they didn't dare to face for fear of his knife.

The honorable *panzerotto*, round and bespectacled as befits a future president of the socialist republic, began to compete with the Bolshevik *sans-culottes* and the sneaky English in the field of espionage. I had no sympathy for him because I would tell him to his face the harshest truths. Boasting of friendships and affiliations with the court of Foggia, he wanted to mooch a hundred lire off a poor woman who lived in misery and had initiated legal proceedings to separate from her husband, a scoundrel and a bully. I, who had gratuitously drawn up the petition of that unfortunate woman, when I learned that Costa, on the strength of a simple recommendation, was demanding money, did not give him anything. *Panzerotto* found out and swore revenge.

To make me jealous, he lured Assuntina to his house,[25] promising her financial compensation and his influential protection as an important man. Then he had his *secretary* tell me that he had called the girl

---

25   The ministry granted him permission to have a private residence. [ENZO]

ENZO MARTUCCI

to provoke me. In response, I assured the *secretary* that before the evening I would break the honorable man's glasses. Costa, upon receiving the message, immediately ran in my direction and denounced me. And the director, who saw me as dogs see cats, had me arrested and, as punishment, transferred to the nearby island of San Domino.

Panzerotto, after a few days, was transferred to Lampedusa and from there he fled abroad. In France, among the exiles, he posed as a victim of fascism and as a hero who had escaped from confinement. But he did not reveal that in Tremiti he had engaged in denunciation and, to his shame, had exposed to police reprisals another confined person who was much more rebellious than him.

SECOND EXILE

After three years, my confinement ended and I returned to Naples. But I only stayed there for four months. The anarchist leader, the seventy-seven-year-old altruist who had been promoting universal brotherhood for half a century, sent me back into isolation as he had sent me to jail in 1920, denying me the means to save myself in France.

Exhausted from the uneven struggle I had been waging for 20 years, I hoped to rest after so many battles and regain some breath. But I made the unforgivable mistake of visiting an old *comrade* whom I had not seen since '32. And this visit cost me another five years of confinement.

The man of universal embrace, emphatic and a simulator, with a heart of gold in words but a heart of lead in deeds, *hugged me* and declared, through tears, that he felt happy to find the *maestro of anarchy* again, "the young but brave fighter who had not bent under the overwhelming storm." Having learned that I was giving private lessons to some high school students to make a living, he wanted me to prepare his son for admission exams to the lyceum. Therefore, I had to go to the dear doctor's house daily, and living in his intimacy, I became even more convinced of what I had already known since '20, that the leader hid under the veil of humanitarianism and utopianism the fierce greed of a famished wolf. All his faintness for others, his exaggerated altruism, his love for the poor people were nothing but a mask that concealed his greedy desire for bread, his insatiable thirst for money. I. posed as an anarchist, a libertarian socialist, a world regenerator, to deceive and shear everyone. Thus, he could eat the money that his American comrades sent him for political victims and propaganda in Naples. Thus, in the time of liberalism, he had secured the support and protection of the Freemasonry. When fascism came, he had raised the tricolor flag on the balcony during national holidays and, during the war in Abyssinia, he had also offered gold to the homeland. However, this did not prevent him, when I saw him again, from cursing Mussolini and his regime with the antifascists who visited him. For fifty years, all those who frequented his house were arrested upon leaving, but he lived undisturbed and had only been in jail once, for a few days. Many said that secretly, he was informing the police. I did not want to believe this rumor and regretted it at my own expense. His lover, who could have been his daughter in age, exploited the dental office staff, mistreated the maids, posed as a despot, a tyrant, a capricious and fierce Messalina. He, the humanitarian, let it slide. The newly affluent peasant woman, who added the arrogance and conceit of a *parvenu* to her domineering nature, slapped the poor servant because she had peeled the potatoes badly and sent her away without paying her. The servant cried, apologized, protested that she could not immediately find another job and begged not to be put on the street. The demagogue's henchwoman, the villager from Lucania, remained immovable and pointed to the door. And he, the altruist, the man with a heart of gold, did not intervene, indeed he approved that the maid was not paid for the services rendered. Then, five minutes later, he began to curse the capitalists who exploit the workers and the fascists who oppress the proletariat.

One evening, at his house, I was discussing with an engineer and saying that, for the individualist, there are only two logical conceptions of life: anarchy or imperialism. The doctor protested; I explained my thoughts.

"The freedom of the individual does not end where that of others begins. It only ends where his force stops. To satisfy my passions or to make my ideas triumph, I must necessarily fight and defeat those who have passions or ideas contrary to mine. If others resist me, if they are individualists like me and do not want to recognize any authority, then an equilibrium is spontaneously produced between the free warring forces. Now one side of the balance tilts, now the other side tilts. Each one develops the maximum power to contain the adversary and there can no longer be any definitive overlaps, stable commands and resigned obediences. This is anarchy. But if instead others give in to the attack, if their herd instinct drives them to bow before the superior man, it is natural that he should exercise his empire over the amorphous mass and use the mass as material for the construction of the masterpiece of his greatness. This is imperialism. Against every despot, in general servitude, rise the few men who do not want to adapt to slavery; but the despot and the rebel are equivalent manifestations of intense, tropical, exuberant life that does not tolerate restraints and limitations. Therefore, anarchy and imperialism are closer than one might think."

"But yours is the morality of force," observed the socialist engineer, scandalized.

"And it is not anarchy," protested the old leader, "anarchy is love, brotherhood, free agreement among men in a perfect and egalitarian society."

"Yes, the anarchy of the friars, of Saint Errico Malatesta and Prince Kropotkin. For it to be achievable, only the passions that morality has agreed to call good would have to exist in humans. But from the dark depths of our nature, from what Dostoevsky calls the underground and Nietzsche the Dionysian depths of the self, different impulses erupt at every moment, driving us towards love or hate, generosity or cruelty, agreement or struggle. The self is a complex and obscure reality, not a simple being, easily knowable and classifiable among social animals. If you remind me, with Aristotle, that man is a political animal, I will answer you by quoting Mandeville's *Fable of the Bees.* Man is social and antisocial depending on the moment, the circumstances, the passions. The self, which wants to subjugate the non-self, sometimes appears in angelic forms, and at other times in the guise of Satan.

"That is why your idyllic dream is a utopia. The impulse for unity, that fundamental biological impulse that Bakunin speaks of, is lacking in the human species."

A socialist lawyer who claimed to be a philosopher and, as such, taught the doctor that Voltaire was an atheist and the historian Buonarroti, brother of Michelangelo, brought his enlightened wisdom to the discussion. He began to show me that man is good by nature, but society makes him bad, and therefore we must transform society and destroy dictators, capitalists, egoists, that is, all those who want evil. Thus, in society, perfect order "already existing in nature" will prevail.

"This is another foolishness," I replied smiling. "Nature is not idyllic, as you believe, nor is it diabolical, as Christians assert. The nature we know phenomenally, that is, in the way that involves the conformation of our senses and intellect, is a collection of different and irreducible facts. It is a reality that embraces, that includes within itself, spirit and matter, cosmos and chaos, order and disorder, harmony and conflict. These elements are all necessary and equivalent: there are no fixed laws that govern them and establish that some must always remain subordinate to the opposites. Therefore, if order now predominates in reality, this does not prevent us from considering the hypothesis that, in the future, nature may change and that, as a result of the movement of balance, the disorder, which today is reduced, may regain the upper hand and drive order into a state of inferiority. The elements are equivalent: I have said it and I repeat it. Either as manifestations of different substances, necessarily or accidentally associated; or as manifestations of a single substance that can only be expressed in opposite forms that are irreducible to unity, as forms, and could not identify themselves except by annihilating themselves or returning to the undifferentiated reality of simple substance. Therefore, it is not understood why among these equivalent elements, all necessary to nature, some should always remain at the forefront, with directive functions, and others should perform the task of obedient and disciplined followers. In the reality we know, and in ourselves who are part of it, order and disorder are revealed side by side, in a state of continuous oscillation. Why do you not want to see the first and ignore the second?"

"Oh, come on, leave the metaphysical subtleties aside," protested the lawyer. "The disorder does not really exist, it is only an illusion of ours. In nature, there is only order, constant and progressive, the eternal rule. Moreover, science shows us that the universe, which has existed for billions of years, has always been ordered."

"Bravo, lawyer!" I replied. "Don't you realize that you are supporting a thesis very close to the teleological one of Thomas Aquinas? But I ask you, entering the field of metaphysics in which you are pushing me: this ordered universe, which has existed for ten, twenty, thirty billion years, where did it come from? From a previous reality, certainly. Well, this previous reality could not have been *absolute nothingness* because from *nothing comes nothing* and no wand of the Almighty could perform the miracle. Therefore, it had to be a relative nothingness, the non-being of *being*, the same actual reality that existed in the opposite way to how it exists now.[26] It was the chaos in which all the elements were turbulently swirling. Then, later, this chaos ordered the confused elements within it and generated a new reality, the universe. But in its ultimate essence, chaos remained chaos, it did not transform but, united with that other part of itself that metamorphosed and became the universe, it now presents us with the spectacle of nature in which being and non-being are side by side, both within and outside of us. For this reason, man never manages to establish harmony in his soul between the opposing tendencies that rage within it. To live

26   This hypothesis is far from inadmissible. Even a Catholic scientist, Sir Edmund Whittaker, concluded his investigations into the age of the world with these words: "These different calculations converge in the conclusion that there was an era, about one or ten billion years ago, before which the cosmos, if it existed, *existed in a form totally different from anything we know*: so that it represents the ultimate limit of science. We may perhaps, without impropriety, refer to it as creation" (*Space and Spirit,* 1946). But since the creation of absolute nothingness is *inconceivable*, it is better to believe that at the origins, reality existed in a way opposite to the current one, that is, as chaos from which the cosmos then emerged. Either by its own inner necessity; or by the ordering action of a demiurgic element (counterbalanced, in eternity, by the action of opposing elements); or by other causes unknown to us and perhaps never knowable. [ENZO]

ENZO MARTUCCI

as one feels means to abandon oneself to the feeling or passion that, at the present moment, appears stronger, subjugating other feelings and passions that, later, will take over. Therefore, if we cannot establish harmony within ourselves, how can we establish it, definitive and perfect, between ourselves and other men, near and far?"

The lawyer and the anarchist leader remained silent. But the peasant woman from Lucania, who had not understood anything of what she had heard, intervened in the discussion declaring that I was "telling stories" and that love, which is the fundamental impulse of human beings, would eventually triumph. Imperatively, with that authoritative tone that made the maids tremble, she pronounced that good had to become mandatory and the proponents of evil, the exploitative bourgeoisie, the fascist murderers who had massacred poor blacks in Abyssinia and the Spanish comrades, had to be all shot. Then Eden would come, the land of milk and honey, the future society of peace and agreement.

At that moment, the maid approached and, showing a terrifyingly swollen foot, asked the lady for permission to go to bed.

"No, because you still have to sweep the living room and wax the floors," the fake peasant replied.

"But, madam, look at my foot. It hurts terribly, and I can no longer bear this pain. If I continue to tire myself, I won't be able to work tomorrow."

"And I'll send you away because those who are here have to earn their bread. If you are sick, go to the hospital. But if you stay at home, you must absolutely do your work."

The poor woman sighed and limped away. I got up feeling nauseous. Addressing the old impostor, I said:

"An amoralist who accepts life without exceptions and recognizes the naturalness and equivalence of passions, good and bad, has compassion for that unfortunate woman and leaves so as not to see her suffer. Your female, who poses as a humanitarian and wants the unconditional triumph of Good, denies rest to a sick person. If the bourgeoisie do not know pity, she knows it less than they do. And all of you, moralists, altruists, utopians, are nothing but a bunch of hypocritical rogues and scoundrels."

I took my hat and left. In the following days, I definitively broke ties with I., whom I was fed up with. The suspicion that he was a spy had been confirmed by new evidence and I didn't want to have any relationship with a person of his kind.

In a letter I sent him to express my contempt, after reminding him of all the baseness he committed, I concluded with this observation:

"All this shows me that you are not an anarchist because, if you were like me, you would behave differently."

The doctor delivered the letter to the police. Immediately, the police conducted a search of my house, seized a copy of my letter to I., and took me to prison. The Provincial Commission of Naples, with an order dated April 25, 1937, imposed five years of political exile on me, for *my profession of anarchist faith*.

And I returned, with handcuffs on my wrists, to Tremiti.

That damned rock, which if I could, I would blow up with dynamite, welcomed me for the second time in its barren womb. And I resumed my former life, a life of boredom, disgust, and repressed rebellions. We, the exiles, could not go down to the port and had to spend the whole day on the top of the barren and inhospitable rock, among the four huts of the village crushed by the imposing antiquity of the medieval castle that overlooks them. And we went up and down, from the houses to the castle and from the castle to the houses, moving in a space that was too narrow and walking on certain sharp stones that pierced the soles of our feet. And every day we could only do that, always seeing the same things, meeting the same people, listening to the hoarse voices of the drunks who sang, "La violetta, la va, la va" and the exasperating speeches of the communists who monotonously repeated, with obligatory words, the praises of Russia and the panegyric of Stalin.

Around us were police officers with hard grit and inquisitive looks, fierce hounds who spied on every gesture and every word, ready to arrest us. Then there were other even more insidious enemies, the exiles who spied or invented slanders against their comrades to gain their own release. The Bolsheviks gathered in small groups, lent each other support, watched each other's backs, and formed a solid bloc against which the police-spy action could have less effect. But those who, like me, were isolated except for the red sect, and against the police and its lackeys, were in the conditions of the slothful in the vestibule of hell: displeasing to God and his enemies. And they received beatings from all sides.

The day was boring. I studied, others conversed or went up and down the castle or hung out in the taverns. At sunset, the trumpet sounded, and we all had to return to the barracks where they locked us up and left us until morning, in the company of the itching caused by bedbugs and the nauseating stench of the latrines.

That was the good life, no doubt about it... Mussolini only gave us six lire a day each. And with such a meager sum we had to live, and it wasn't enough to pay for the garbage they gave us to eat in the cafeteria or Ciociò's tavern. But the communist leaders arranged themselves differently. With the money from the Red Aid.[27] And, long live Stalin, life was not too hard for them.

The Bolshevik sect, at the time of my return to Tremiti, had become more numerous and dominant. Some sectarians continued to spy on the director, not

---

27   "Soccorso Rosso" refers to an international so-
cial-service organization. Founded in 1922 by the Communist
International to function as an "international political Red
Cross", providing material and moral aid to radical "class-war"
political prisoners around the world.

ENZO MARTUCCI

only to gain personal benefits but also on behalf of the "party", to better strike the political opponents with the weapon of denunciation. But the sect, officially, maintained an oppositional, legalistic and formal attitude towards the authority of the island constituted by police who had been corrupted by fascism. Director Fusco took umbrage at such an attitude, which practically consisted of inducing the confined to resign themselves to the regime of confinement combined with the useless ostentation of certain forms of passive protest. He was the most beautiful type of presumptuous idiot I have ever known. The same one who sent me to punishment on S. Domino when I wanted to break the glasses of the honorable Costa.

Fusco, who physically resembled a jack-in-the-box, with two little mustaches turned upwards and certain eyes that emitted bursts of vanity, could not tolerate that the Bolshevik soldiers did not greet him when they met him on the street. He didn't understand that it was a tactic, and that the same truculent Stalinists who publicly showed indifference or contempt for him, thus demonstrating that they had not submitted, when they were alone, entered his office and groveled and flattered to make amends for their fault. The poor fool understood nothing. He didn't realize that those who prevented escape attempts, individual revolts, and even the riots of the many, driven by despair, were Graziadei, Vincenzi, and the other Stalinist sergeants who preached patient waiting for the great day of revenge, as a result of international politics. And in the meantime, they forced their followers, who were the majority of the exiles, to submit to all kinds of oppression, only expressing with well-behaved gestures a restrained moral and social disapproval. Fusco, blinded by his megalomania as a semi-literate gendarme, was not satisfied with discipline, but wanted slavery and recantation. And he decreed that the exiles had to salute him and his agents Roman-style at the daily roll call.

This *ukase* (edict) provoked general indignation. Even the donkey, when it's beaten too much, ends up kicking, and the police provocation momentarily awakened the exiles of Tremiti. Everyone was agitated and the communists and anarchists immediately declared that they would rebel against the injunction.

"We will not salute and they cannot report us because the public security law does not require us to raise our hand," they declared.

"But," I replied, "the director will inflict so many reprimands and punishments on us that, in the end, everyone will get tired and, sooner or later, capitulate. Passive resistance, Gandhism, will mark our defeat. Therefore, if we do not want to endure the imposition, we have no other way than to rise up suddenly, disarm the few agents who attend the roll call, surprise-occupy the three police barracks in which we will encounter little resistance from the attackers who, not suspecting the revolt, will not be ready to face it. At the same time, another group will occupy the telegraph office and destroy the equipment. Since there is no radio transmitter station or any other means of communication on Tremiti, apart from the telegraph, the news of the uprising will not immediately reach Italy, and reinforcements will not be sent. We, the masters of the island, will wait for the arrival of the steamboat that is due to arrive from Manfredonia tomorrow, seize it, and sail towards Dalmatia. The plan has a good chance of success, given the weak force here and the surprise that will be our best ally. We will regain our freedom and deal a heavy blow to those who have deprived us of it. Moreover, even if an unforeseen event will make the plot fail, we will perish but fighting and returning the blows."

The communist leaders and anarchists rejected the proposal, which they called crazy. They searched for all kinds of excuses, pointed out all the dangers, even the most remote and least likely, to prove that the revolt would fail. So in 1920, they presented all the difficulties to continuously postpone the revolution; so every time there was an action to be taken, they always found a plausible excuse to back out. Some people like to plot and work in the shadows, but not face danger openly, in the light of day. The Bolsheviks know how to challenge exile and imprisonment, but not death. They are too attached to their *own hides* to become heroes. They think that one can return from the island, and come out of prison with the halo of martyrdom and with a greater chance of becoming a great or small Stalin of the next dictatorship. But death is the end of every hope: it must therefore be avoided. The communist wants to live to eat and to command. Command is not for him, as it is for the Nietzschean Superman, a means to intoxicate oneself, to realize a superb dream of personal greatness; but it is a bestial lust for oppression, a tiger-like desire to grip, to impose one's own dominion, one's own fanaticism, one's own barbarism, satisfying all the instincts and appetites of the brute.

The next day, at roll call, there was a banal exchange of punches between the exiles and the police, but it did not go any further. The management ordered a hundred arrests; those left outside hurried to say goodbye. The Bolshevik leaders, with lawyer Corrado Graziadei at the head, did not raise their arm in the Roman salute, so as not to discredit themselves among their followers; but they saluted by taking off their hats. Instead, a few rebels did not make any salute, and I was among them. Arrested and locked up in a large cell to serve our aggravated sentence, we remained, in a Gandhian way, in inertia, at the instigation of the communist leaders who had been imprisoned with us. The heat suffocated us, the lack of air gave the torments of asphyxia, a young Stalinist, already suffering from tuberculosis, died after 15 days, and the red generals continued to preach calm and passive resistance. Sickened by that foolish comedy that led to no results, after serving my month of punishment, I separated from the Gandhi-like rebels. The Bolsheviks criticized me harshly, but after a few days, their leader, lawyer Graziadei, saluted in the Roman way, to save himself. And he was acquitted of exile. Instead, I remained relegated and transferred from Tremiti to Ventottenne.

In the island that Settembrini remembers in his

ENZO MARTUCCI

Reminiscences, I found greater police rigor and a more serious opposition between Bolsheviks and the leadership. The more the police tightened their grip, the more the Marxists closed ranks, stiffened discipline, exacerbated sectarianism and ferocity. Many followers deserted, frightened by the severity of the police or nauseated by the tyranny of the red leaders; and these, furious at the daily abandonments, demanded blind obedience from the faithful and poisoned, with hydrophobic rage, the calumny, boycott, and persecution of non-Stalinists. When a new prisoner arrived at Ventottenne, the communists immediately surrounded him, drew him into their orbit, dictated the norm of conduct and the rule of thought. Three or four propagandists subjected him to continuous injections of Moscow doctrine, the implacable censors, in charge of the supervision and direction of the neophytes, accompanied him everywhere, in the barracks, on the streets, at roll call, explaining to him the duty and necessity of joining the party and conforming to its discipline, and showing him the advantages he would derive from it and the damage he would receive by opposing the strongest group in the confinement. The new arrival, stunned, harassed, and suggested, gave in; and from that moment on, he became part of the army of the *most devoted and loyal*, the human machines that felt, wanted, and acted as the Bolshevik high command dictated.

But if the neophyte resisted, if he did not let himself be absorbed and maintained his independence, the most bitter persecution was unleashed against him. The communists passed on the password and tried, by all means, to make his life impossible. No one spoke to him, no one approached him, everyone expressed contempt and aversion towards him. The adjectives "spy", "Manchurian", were whispered in his ear at every moment. The most painful isolation and the harshest contempt weighed on the outcast, humiliated him, crushed him. In the dormitory and in the mess hall, everyone tried to annoy him in every way, to mortify him, to offend him. The poor man swallowed poison, chewed bitterness, writhed under the iron heel that weighed on his chest, then ended up capitulating. The police kept telling him that if he joined the communists, he would never return home; but he lived there, in that environment, he could not resign himself for long to the shame of being a reprobate, a leper, he could not bear that his companions always spat in his face and treated him like a filthy thing. Therefore, even at the cost of ruining himself even more and of delaying his return to his family, he had to become a communist. If he resisted for so long, if he showed his teeth to the bullies, then they devised other means; someone, in his absence, hid in his bunk an object belonging to a Bolshevik; then the owner reported to the police the disappearance of the object. The agents carried out searches in all the bunks of the dormitory, found the evidence in that of the poor unsuspecting person and arrested him for theft. The police were deceived and the non-conformist was punished.

Despite this, many abandoned the communists

ENZO MARTUCCI

but, after a short time, they were released or trans-ferred elsewhere; the Stalinists, on the other hand, always remained in Ventotenese, constituted a compact, organized, disciplined group, possessed a surplus of numbers, and managed to dominate the confinement and boycott those who did not submit to their yoke.

No one spoke, no one protested against the abuses of the Bolsheviks: the power of fear silenced everyone. There were spies, but communist coun-terintelligence paralyzed their actions and ensured that the most serious events did not reach the ears of those who confided in the police. Stalin's follow-ers acted with such cunning mastery that only rarely did the police manage to catch them in the act. But even when something was discovered, it was the min-ions, the executors who fell; the leaders gave orders and remained in the shadows, pushing others for-ward but not personally compromising themselves, thus making themselves invulnerable. They had informants who daily reported everything that was said and done on the island; they commanded loy-al soldiers who obeyed with sheep-like submission, whether it was to donate money to the Red Cross or to persecute non-communists, or whether they had to protest against the leadership or create an infamy to ruin someone. And the generals, the big shots, the red eminences, pulling the strings behind the scenes, acted like Stalin. Was there an enemy to be beaten? They sent their armed men. Did they want to spread a slander against an unwelcome person? They spread the word and, in a moment, the swarm of followers had spread the rumor. Did they want to file a complaint with the ministry attacking the police? They dictated it and a foolish X signed it, drawing on himself the resentment and ill will of the police. The docile minions deprived themselves of cigarettes to pay the mandatory fee to the Red Cross, and the leaders, with that money, drank tea, ate jam, stuffed themselves with cream and chicken, and offered vermouth to the three or four Theroigne de Méricourts,[28] at a reduced rate, who represented female communism in the Ventotenian era. For the greatness of Stalin and the redemption of humanity, the soldiers fasted and the generals feasted. *Ad majorem dei gloriam.*[29]

Among the leaders stood out the figure of the limping snail, the Turin native Roveda, a martyr in Italy and abroad due to his past imprisonments, and therefore adored. His ridiculous arrogance was combined with the plebeian arrogance of the indivisible companion Vincenzo Baldazzi, former commander, under Mingrino's orders, of the Arditi del Popolo and a Stalinist in the interest of the Popular Front and his own ambition. This stocky Don Quixote recalled, with his determination, the fierce sonnet with

---

28   Théroigne de Méricourt (1762–1817) was a leading advocate for women's rights during the French Revolution. Born Anne-Josèphe Terwagne in Belgium, she gained prominence for her impassioned speeches and writings promoting gender equality. Despite her notable contributions, her radical views led to persecution and imprisonment.

29   "For the greater glory of God", the motto of the Society of Jesus, an order of the Catholic Church.

which Rapisardi portrayed Carducci in the memorable polemic between the two writers: "In canine face, pig-like eye." He was the true type of a people's leader, an insolent, presumptuous, vulgar Masaniello. He told everyone about the victories of the good old days when, at the head of his brave men, he defeated the fascists and slapped the consuls of the militia in the midst of their legions. Listening to him, it was incomprehensible how Mussolini could have entered Rome, but he explained the mystery with the stupidity of Facta, who had not wanted to entrust him with... the strongholds of the city.

Friend of Roveda and perhaps more sectarian and talkative than his communist allies, he was an authority among the confinements in Ventottenne, who saluted the future generalissimo of the Italian Red Army with the beret of authority on his head. Beside him and the Bolshevik saint, at a respectful distance of three steps, appeared the accountant Calogero Barcellona, a valuable deputy, with the composure and regularity of a bank employee who had spent his entire life in Milan economizing on a salary of 500 lire per month. A little behind, according to the hierarchical order, was "Frater" Caprioli, small, elusive, hypocritical, a true type of Dominican from the Inquisition and a fanatical superintendent of the auto-da-fé. And at his side, martial and *indomitable* as befits the attendant of General Baldazzi, marched Alfonso Failla, a barber from Syracuse, intelligent and self-taught but mafia, oppressive and ambitious, who claimed and still claims to be an anarchist but cooked up anarchy with all the sauces in the hope of becoming *someone*.

These were the members of the Bolshevik high command that directed political confinements on the island of Ventotene. They were the tyrants of those poor devils who had the pretense of rebelling, with actions or with words, against Mussolini, only to become the humble slaves of five despotic and demanding nobodies.

Naturally, I immediately told the generals and soldiers what I felt. I called the leaders "*cardboard Stalins*" and the followers "*sheep with curved horns.*" The accountant Barcellona, who slept in the same room as me, became the target of the fierce barbs my sarcasm launched at him. When I saw his attendant every evening, a certain Stokovic, from Trieste, who, in homage to communist discipline, made his bed, prepared his tea, and took the beatings without responding, I asked the authoritarian Calogero why he didn't get himself a chamber pot that his faithful servant could empty in the morning. The Bolshevik leaders wanted to command in the barracks and mess halls, not only imposing themselves on their followers but on everyone. They established the time at which confinements had to wake up, the time for study, and the time for rest. They wanted to turn confinement into a barracks and be its corporals. Everyone obeyed, and I was the only one who showed his teeth.

The first morning that the Moscow squires woke me up, inviting me to get up, I grabbed a shoe and declared that I would break the glasses of the accountant

Barcellona if I was not left alone. But my anarchist in-difference sharpened the hatred that the Communists had for me and did not succeed in waking the others up. Sixty centuries of gregarious life have transformed men into sheep and any example, any exhortation, is useless in awakening in their hearts personal pride and a sense of independence. Stubborn to the point of nausea, the Marxist sheep continued to obey the leaders supinely, endured rebukes and punishments, were locked up in the barracks with a ban on leaving and adhered to the order not to speak for a given time with a comrade who had been subjected to a solemn punishment. They were like so many puppets whose strings were pulled by various Bonellis, Rovedas, or Baldazzis, that is, by various little bosses who trained in the exercise of Stalinist authority. The Communist, consumed by the lust for command, servilely obeys his superior, waiting for the day when he can climb a rung in the party hierarchy and take his place. Thus Stokovic made Barcelona's bed dreaming of the day when someone else would make his bed. Thus Franzoni, in Tremiti, left his wife alone at home with the general who had gone to visit her and thought that, in the future, with the Greek on his cap, he would also visit the comrades' wives.

As the relations between me and the communists became increasingly tense, I learned that Roveda, the hero, the martyr, the symbol of Bolshevik resis-tance, had secretly submitted a plea for clemency to the government, a real act of submission in which he praised Mussolini and the regime, dating it with the 15th year of the Fascist Era. Disgusted by the hypocrisy of that saint who preached intransigence and urged others to stay on the front lines, while secretly seeking to save himself by reciting the comedy of repentance, I shared the news with everyone: "This is what the communists are like," I declared, "cowardly and hypocritical. They impose inflexibility, label and persecute those who bend, hurl the most ferocious insults and make life impossible for those poor devils without ideas and without a political past who, by mistake, end up here and invoke the mercy of the dictator; then, unbeknownst to everyone, they too submit pleas for clemency and return home without the audience seeing their pants fall. For the masses, they remain pure, indomitable, but they have secretly asked Mussolini for forgiveness."

When I interrogated Roveda before revealing his defection, he could not deny having asked the Duce for release from confinement. But he sought pretexts to attenuate his act and walked away chewing bitter thoughts; then, with the perfidy and hypocrisy which are special talents of the communists, he ordered his followers to launch the most disgusting campaign of slander and infamy against me. Baldazzi, the Roman Masaniello, the degraded general of the Arditi del Popolo, took charge of the attack. Failla, the anarchist from Moscow, Baldazzi's attendant, stood by his superior and passed him the poisoned arrows that were supposed to strike me. Accustomed to kissing the hand of communist allies who have slaughtered his libertarian comrades in Russia and Spain, but who will give him the staff of command in his native Syracuse when Baffone comes, the Sicilian barber sought to pierce me in every way with the vile weapon of defamation, even though until the day before he had declared himself my friend. The discipline of the popular front imposed the struggle against me, even though he knew I was unquestionably right; but sectarianism, Baldazzi's influence, the need for agreement with the Bolshevik leaders with whom he has always been closely associated, in Ponza and elsewhere, urged him to unleash furious attacks that barely scratched the surface.

Following the generals, the brainless and will-less sheep-like followers, the docile fools who believe everything their superiors say and act supinely as commanded, attempted to boycott me, obeying the order from above. In order to isolate me, they persuaded or threatened as many confined individuals as possible not to speak with me. They invented the strangest stories and the lowest slanders about me, which they whispered in ears secretly. They tried to exasperate me with the most vile insults and the most treacherous maneuvers, and one of them, who swaggered in the infirmary as the doctor's assistant, went so far as to deny me the medicines that were rightfully mine with the most stupid excuses. The action squad organized an assault that was to take place as follows: at night, while I was sleeping, four thugs were to approach my bed and, throwing a blanket over my head, beat me. At the last minute, a counter-order arrived, and the attack was postponed: the entire confinement and even the administration were aware of my campaign against Roveda and the counter-campaign that the Communists were conducting for revenge. If I had been beaten and injured, everyone would have assumed that the Bolshevik leaders were the ones who ordered it and would have been compromised. Fearing the danger, they stopped their hands, already ready to strike.

In those days, while the subversive action of the Stalinists was attempting to stab me in the back, an individual who claimed to be an anarchist but was actually a spy took off his mask with me and confided that, having infiltrated among the Communists and become aware of all their schemes (hidden weapons, clandestine correspondence, etc.), he would report them to the administration. He also told me that, at the behest of Failla and Baldazzi, he had stolen a notebook from me in which the members of the Popular Front suspected that I was writing the anti-Bolshevik book I had announced. Baldazzi, having received the notebook and paid ten lire in compensation to the thief-spy, was disappointed to find, instead of political criticism, only notes on Lange's *History of Materialism*. In his gross ignorance, he had not understood much of it and had deferred to Failla, who was supposed to explain it to him.

Referring to all these details and his intention to denounce the communists, the pseudo-anarchist, who was already a confidant of the police in Genoa, believed that I kept silent because, ultimately, he wanted to strike my fiercest enemies. He wanted to strike them, of course, in the hope of being released from exile that the ministry would have granted him; but, apart from that, he was avenging me as well and I was supposed to help him by giving a literary form to the written statement he intended to send to the management.

Instead, I called "brother" Caprioli and informed him of everything. I hate communists, I'm always ready to confront them, but I fight openly, fairly, and I don't want even my most bitter opponents to be hit from behind. In this book, I could tell things far more serious than those about the Bolsheviks, but by doing so, I would indirectly denounce someone and therefore I refrain from doing it.

When I learned that a spy was about to sell those who slandered me and fought me with the vilest weapons, I warned them and saved them. I acted in this way out of chivalry, for the same feeling that, in Paris, drove me to protect an unknown woman, in the Place de la Nation café, at the risk of my life, and that spurred me to defend the fascist Neri against false witnesses in Tremiti. As a response to my generosity, the communist snakes intensified their campaign of defamation against me and provoked and attacked two anarchists, Francesco Ticchi and Amedeo Bassi, who agreed with me.

The charlatan Roveda did not give up but, practically, applied the lessons of sectarianism and Jesuitism he received from his superior, the pontiff Gramsci. On which it would be appropriate to read what the old and daring anarchist Paolo Schicchi, who was in prison with him, wrote about him. And he said a lot of bad things about him.

STILL IN HELL

In the years that followed, my life continued to unfold in loneliness and pain.

From Ventotene, I was transferred to Macchiagodena, a remote village in the mountains of Molise.

From the *friendly* environment of the fanatical communists who slandered me, I moved to the equally welcoming environment of the peasants, rude and *ignorant*, who, incited by the local priest, sent their children to throw stones at the anarchist, an *enemy of God*. The story lasted until I thoroughly beat one of those rascals. I then ran the risk of ending up in jail, but the consequence was that, when I passed by, stones no longer flew.

From Macchiagodena, the ministry moved me to Isernia where I served the last two years of my confinement. I found a certain tranquility in this town and was able to devote myself again to my preferred philosophical and literary studies. In 1942, I finished my period of exile and finally returned to Naples.

But I couldn't remain inactive in the singing city. I had been too fiercely struck, too harshly offended, for my rebellious soul to resign itself to what had happened and not seek revenge. I secretly formed a revolutionary action group and planned to blow up the headquarters of the fascist federation with a time bomb. One of my companions, the traitor Datodi, denounced me and the others a few days before the attack was to take place. We were arrested, but since there was no evidence and legal action could not be taken against us, the head of the OVRA,[30] Pastore, forced me, with the threat of inflicting harm on my sick mother, to sign a confession. However, as soon as I was transferred to jail, I denied the signature, declaring to the investigating judge that it had been extracted by force. Therefore, the others were released and I remained alone inside, following a new accusation lodged against me by the embittered Pastore.

The detention lasted for eight months. They were eight months of physical and moral pain, suffered in the oppressive gloom of a dark cell where I had no company other than my dark thoughts. I was released at the end of September 1943 when the people rebelled against the Germans and had four days of fighting.

Breathing the free air, I realized that if my body felt exhausted from the torments of prison, my spirit, on the other hand, burned, consumed by the same rebellious fire that, at 16, had driven me to promote an uprising in Vigevano.

Now fascism had fallen, and I hoped it would drag the entire bourgeois society, the society that had

---

30   Organization for Vigilance and Repression of Antifascism, the Italian secret police.

been persecuting me for 23 years, into the abyss of its guilt, and I wanted to see its inglorious death. And to give it death, to plunge the knife into its throat, I felt spurred on by the hatred that had been simmering inside me for so long, by the frenzied need to avenge my youth wasted in confinement and in jail and my dreams shattered by poverty and persecution.

But I could not destroy the enemy alone; I needed the support of others. And I hoped that, at least at that moment, I would not be lacking in it.

Instead, I had to be disappointed: fascism disappeared, but bourgeois society remained. Mussolini and some of the hierarchy were executed, and the regime was shattered. But the bourgeoisie, who had kept fascism in power for over four decades, rushed to don the democratic cloak and were left in command by the conquering Americans of Italy.

The fat industrialists of the North and the haughty landowners of the South, the solemn big shots of the bureaucracy and the burly police managers, all those who had fornicated with fascism, who had enriched themselves with the leader, and who had paid the lowest services to the leader for twenty-three years, found themselves, *ipso facto*, through transformational *fregolianism*,[31] antifascists of the first hour.

Abandoning their ally, shamelessly exploited, at the moment when it collapsed under the blows of the foreigner, the Italian bourgeoisie rushed in front of the Yankee trucks to shine the shoes of the soldiers from across the Atlantic and reveal to the black

31

shirts their burning love for freedom and hatred for the tyrant.

Of likable people in Italy, only those few who still had the courage not to renounce themselves, defying the Stalinist thugs' bullet to the back of the neck and the concentration camp set up by the Anglo-Saxons, remained.

As before, during the fascist era, there had been only a few, very few, likable men: the antifascists who, by standing up against the dictatorship, had faced imprisonment and confinement. But the Italian bourgeoisie, taken as a whole, gave the most miserable spectacle of belly-flopping and cowardice, of betrayal and cowardice. Those who had eaten with fascism now spat in the plate of the food they had consumed and prostituted themselves to the new master. Those who had received Mussolini's salaries and favors flaunted their democracy and continued to command and devour. To them were added the heroes of the last day, the Platonic antifascists who, during the disreputable 20-year period, had prudently stayed abroad without facing imprisonment and confinement, but who came to Italy with the Moroccan bayonets and the Zanzibar scimitars to demand compensation for the *sacrifices they endured*. So the rare remaining cheese in the beautiful country was put to the test by the sharp teeth of these hungry mice, who already despised the gruel of an Italian prison for the best meals consumed on the tables of Parisian restaurants and paid for with the money of the Masonic Lodge or the Communist Party or even the agents of the OVRA, of which many exiles were secret informants.

The priests, who emerged from the sacristy and had their own scores to settle with Italy, such as the breach of Porta Pia and the confiscation of church property, joined the bourgeoisie and demagogues in their *general feasting*. They too demanded to have their stomachs filled. And so, gathered around the table, the converted fascists and antifascists from the boulevards, the reverends in Phrygian caps and the disheveled Masaniello, all found themselves in agreement. Eating and drinking, they founded the new antifascism, partisan and opportunist, of which the *most shining* expression became Pietro Nenni, who, upon returning from exile and obtaining the position of High Commissioner for sanctions against fascism, had all the files of the OVRA handed over to him and returned some of them, arousing suspicion that he had wanted to conceal those that revealed his secret connections with Mussolini's political police.

Nenni's communist friends and protectors also participated in the banquet and governmental farce. Their first task was to accept all the renegade fascists into the party, to spin the best idyll with the bourgeoisie who had switched from Mussolini to Roosevelt, and to restrain and lull the proletariat, this eternal donkey that, following 20 years of repression and the suffering of war, had briefly awakened from its millennial torpor and seemed determined to make a revolution. But a socialist revolution in Italy at that time would not have been useful to the master

Stalin, who, according to agreements made with the Anglo-Saxon allies, had to prevent any subversive movement in the West, in exchange for freedom of action and domination in the Balkan Peninsula and Danubian Basin. Therefore, the faithful servants of the Little Father, the zealous executors of Moscow's orders, tamed the recalcitrant donkey, returned its reins, and then delivered it into the hands of the bourgeoisie, saying, "*pull as hard as you want, but on the condition that we pull together with you.*"

Don Palmiro Togliatti, the number one Jesuit, the skillful maneuverer who had taken on the task of presenting Bolshevism with a humanist mask, came to Italy, by command of the Mustached God, and began to preach that the Tamerlane regime was not a dictatorship but freedom, not barbarism but civilization, not the negation of the individual but the implementation of progress (with a capital P). He told us all the nonsense he wanted, he said that communism accepts private property, recognizes religion, respects tradition, idolizes democracy and wants, yes, to conquer power for the good of the people, but not with revolutionary means from which it recoils, but with the voluntary suffrage of conscious voters. Never was a wolf hidden under the sheep's clothing so fox-like as the plump, bespectacled politician sent by the modern Genghis Khan among the people of Ausonia. Making a bow to the right and a smile to the left, a wink on one side and a meaningful gesture on the other, this good tracker managed to deceive everyone and to serve, on the dot, the interests of Mr.

Stalin. He said to the bourgeoisie: "Keep me and my shoeshine boy Pietro Nenni as ministers with you. Share the government with the two of us. In return, we will prevent revolution, administering a little opium to the proletariat and allowing the rich to keep their fortune." He secretly confided in the proletariat: "We cannot make the revolution because the Americans are in Italy. Let's pretend to collaborate with the bourgeoisie, let's go to power with them, and then, when we feel stronger, at the right moment, we will trip up the priests and capitalists and establish the communist government."

Thus fooling everyone, promising factories and land to workers and peasants, and offering the bourgeoisie salvation from a thwarted revolution, and to the Church the approval of the Lateran Pacts, the crafty little guy carried out with great zeal the orders of the motorized Tamerlane, who from the imperial castle of the Kremlin greeted him as "leader of the Italian people".

But since not all doughnuts come out with a hole, it so happened that to the coarse Machiavellianism of the diligent Palmiro, the bourgeoisie and the clergy opposed a more subtle, more skilful Machiavellianism, which did not draw its inspiration from the coarseness of the Mongols, but from the fine cunning of the Vatican. They pretended to believe all the lies he told, kept him and Nenni in their Christian Democrat governments, used the two demagogues to restrain the masses, to calm them, to stifle their revolutionary aspirations by diluting them in the little contentments of future promises. Then, at the right moment, when they saw that the crowd had once again been tamed and felt well protected by the reorganized state and the reconstituted police, the bourgeoisie and the clergy gently took Don Palmiro and Don Pietro by the ear and pulled them down from their ministerial armchairs. Then the two gentlemen became opponents again and, unable to speak of revolution, began to declaim that paradise on earth would be brought on the tips of Tartar bayonets and Cossack whips sent, in the near future, by Little Father Stalin, who had broken off with the Anglo-American allies and with Italy ruled by the Christian Democratic clergy in the meantime.

And now, as I write, the comedy continues. And there are still so many foolish workers who believe the lies that these swindlers peddle. Not understanding that if the Italian proletariat remains under the yoke and clerical and bourgeois exploitation, it is because the Marxists have twice betrayed and failed a revolution that was possible: in 1920 and in 1945.

I, having been released from prison, did not resign myself to the evidence. However, even acknowledging that society was not collapsing and that everyone was striving to keep it upright, I attacked it alone. Using my oratory skills, I traveled through central and northern Italy, giving many lectures in which I denounced priests, bourgeois and communists, and urged the crowds to revolutionary destruction. I knew very well that the masses would not respond to the call and that politicians would unite against me, making my life impossible. However, I didn't care; I wanted at least the satisfaction of attacking the hated society and its supporters, exposing its lies, mocking its principles, and revealing its corruption. Even at the cost of ruining myself further, I wanted to vent the anger accumulated in my heart and skewer the hypocrites, spit on the demagogues, attack the opportunists, and the comedians of all colors who pretended to be champions of the established order.

I succeeded in my intention, hitting from all sides, making several big shots bite the dust, defeated in the contradictions; but as a result, I couldn't find employment, and every attempt to earn a living was thwarted by powerful enemies who acted in the shadows. I was reduced to the darkest poverty and forced to live, with my young partner Renata Latini, in the cold and unhealthy attic of a Florentine inn where we skipped meals almost every day. I suffered the most atrocious moral and material tortures, writhing in the spasms of worries and anxieties that poverty generates, feeling a thousand times that my nerves could no longer withstand the extreme tension to which that terrible condition forced them. If it hadn't been for the fear of leaving my partner alone and defenseless, I would have let myself be killed, striking out desperately. But the idea of surrendering or submitting to be allowed to live never crossed my mind. Cowards advised me to back down from my rebellious attitude against everything and everyone; even my mother repeated it to me many times, but I always rejected such advice and remained in my place. Because it was not possible for me to deny myself and renounce my past and my ideas. It was not possible for me to pretend and bow down before that society that had been striking me for 30 years. And finally, because those born with the nature of a lion cannot change it to that of a fox or a sheep.

Alone, without means, and without friends, fought by everyone, misunderstood and slandered, I remained upright under the storm that raged. The only ones who should have stood by my side and supported my revolt would have been those who in Italy profess to be anarchists. Instead, as in the past, they were treacherous and venomous enemies and launched against me the most evil calumnies, hoping to provide other weapons to the many who were fighting against me.

Jealousy, envy, and emptiness; these are the reasons that led to the attack by these sectarians. In fact, for the most part, they are presumptuous and ignorant little people who hate anyone who is worth more than they are. They call themselves anarchists to distinguish themselves from the masses and *put on airs*, but in reality, they have the same herd mentality as the masses, so much so that they present themselves organized in a ridiculous little party, the FAI,[32] led by four or five bosses who are worshipped like saints. And they obtain the veneration of the base

---

32   *Federazione Anarchica Italiana.*

because they are made of the same stuff.

Unscrupulous in words and pose, these self-proclaimed anarchists, on the other hand, retain all the common prejudices and have even gone so far as to be scandalized because in my books *Più Oltre* and *La Bandiera dell'Anticristo* I defended the principles of sexual freedom. While a convinced Catholic, Professor Luigi Scremin, in his work *La questione delle case chiuse*, after quoting some passages from *La Bandiera dell'Anticristo*, honestly acknowledged:

"When, conceptually, one makes sensation the end of the function, that is what one comes to, even if one cannot then translate it into the practice of associated life."

Deadly foes of individualists, who are the sole and true anarchists, the factionalists of the FAI, particularly despise me because, from 1920 onwards, I have consistently labeled their practice and theory as anti-anarchist. And I have demonstrated that the very philosophy of Bakunin, Kropotkin, Malatesta, whom they claim to be adherents of, leads to an organized socialism that is not anarchist. Because the society that derives from it is without government as a conformist mass, in which everyone being equal, they all move in the same way and therefore do not need a leader to command and discipline them. But the original individual who is oppressed by the mass, which wants to impose conformity on him, is subject to a government, that of the number, and therefore is not anarchic in the anarchist society.

On the other hand, some of the current theorists

of libertarian communism, such as Pier Carlo Masini, even more completely resolve anarchy into a democratic system and declare that in the future Commune, even if there will not be almost absolute uniformity, the majority will always have to dictate law to the minority. So, 17 will be right against five in any case, just because they will be 17. And this even if the five are named Goethe, Heine, Nietzsche, Baudelaire, Rimbaud; and the 17 will be distinguished as four dog-catchers, seven sweepers, two public toilet attendants, three cigarette butt collectors, and an intellectual from Masini's school.

Anarchism, on the other hand, is something very different. It is individualism. If it could be realized on a universal scale, it would produce the collapse of every organized society, the return to nature, and the birth of the unique individual, free from all chains. And if instead the rebellion of a few indomitable, freedom-thirsty individuals will remain eternal, against all social orders that succeed each other in time, it will prevent these orders from establishing the absolute conformity they tend towards and from destroying the personality and autonomous life of the individual.

It is true that the influences of the mechanical industrial civilization that oppresses us increasingly develop collectivism and uniformity, and level men, naturally different, into the indistinguishable mass. Today it is even more difficult than in the past to find an outlier. There are no more great tyrants or great rebels. Tyrants do not resemble Alexander, Caesar, or

Napoleon and do not conquer power by employing their exceptional qualities, performing prodigious actions, and exposing themselves to great dangers; but they are vulgar crowd-pleasers, mediocre nobodies, who rise by flattery and adulation of the masses, prostrating themselves at their feet and then crushing them after they have brought them up.[33] And the servile mass esteems and praises them all the more as these leaders trample and exploit them to a greater extent. No one rebels, and if someone, rarely, rises up, they do so within the limits allowed by the law and to obtain a wage increase from the boss. While the great rebels of the past, from Spartacus to Bonnot, have fought for the conquest of all liberties, for the overthrow of every master, and have heroically fallen with the weapon held tightly in their fist.

However, precisely because conformity has increased and individuality is disappearing, it would be necessary to strengthen individualist rebellion in anarchist thought and action as a reaction to social compression. Instead, today's anarchists are increasingly trying to resolve anarchism into a communist form that, from the current organized federation, tends to extend into a future society in which conformity, absolute or almost, will be ensured by greater conformity or by rigid self-discipline exercised by each individual, or more easily by the oppressive predominance of the majority over the minority. Thus,

---

33   Like Stalin, an astute and bloody tyrant but devoid of genius, who managed to seize power under the pretext of liberating the people and serving their interests. [ENZO]

even anarchy, degenerated by the work of degenerate anarchists, has become an element of suffocation for the individual and a denial of freedom that cannot exist in the herd.

And so, faced with such a sad prospect, the question suggested by anguish arises spontaneously:

"What to do?"

"Nothing," reason answers, "let it go, let it pass. We must resign ourselves to the inevitable, withdraw from the struggle, remain in the clutches of the current society and then, when it falls, submit to the whip of its heir, Bolshevism, which will reduce men even more to slavery."

But the heart rebels against this cold demonstration provided by reason that ascertains it glacially. Because the heart cannot stifle its dearest, most intensely felt feelings, it cannot destroy that impulse of revolt that drives the non-gregarious man to break out against the yoke, even when he knows he will not be able to overthrow it and will instead shatter his head in the clash. And I, who follow my feelings more than reason, remain in my place, waiting for death.

Perhaps I will remain alone, as in the past. Perhaps a few men, scattered in space and like me refractory and cursed by the flock, will respond to the call of the distant brother who urges them to battle and the supreme challenge.

But, whatever happens, alone or not, I will never turn back, nor will I ever regret. And if the bourgeois world will always find me an enemy, the monstrous beast advancing from Asia will meet me on its way, armed with fierce hatred and ready to attack it with the same determination with which Sigfrid faced the devouring dragon.

LET'S CRUSH BOLSHEVISM

I do not believe, with Windelband, that there exists a normal conscience that places and fixes absolute values above the relativity of individual valuations and the morality of individual peoples. I do not believe, with Paulsen, in the necessity of a normal type of human or human life that constitutes the measure for the appreciation of the value of actions and qualities. Instead, I accept diversity and different attitudes, and in the contrasting manifestations of existence and in the singularity of thoughts and conduct, I admire the richness of reality and its fruitful production of genuine types and antinomic valuations.

However, there is a way of understanding life that, in my opinion, does not have the right to citizenship in the multitude of ethical forms and conflicting judgments: it is the Bolshevik way, the way that reduces man to animality, indeed to materialistic automatism, and deprives him of all feeling and passion.

The lifeless entity, the wooden object that will dwell in the symmetrical city of the future communist society, eludes any moral classification and repulses every conscience. Francis of Assisi is understandable: he responds to a human sentiment, pity. Friedrich Nietzsche is also understandable; he responds to another sentiment, the will to power. But the puppet that neither loves nor hates, and that is not driven by any good or bad impulse, and is not attracted, as Dostoevsky says, either by the ideal of Sodom or that of the Madonna, but lives mechanically to produce and consume, evades humanity and is inconceivable in the vegetable world.

The morals of generosity and renunciation coexist with the morals of struggle, conquest, and aggression because they respond to the different tendencies of our nature, and it is not possible to create a unique morality or a single type of man without impoverishing life by reducing it to one of its multiple aspects.

However, an appreciation of actions that ignores feelings, the impulses of the soul, the torments of the heart and is based solely on physiological needs and their material expression takes us beyond the limits of our reality, beyond anthropology and zoology, into the domain of botany. Communist morality aspires to the creation of the automatic man, devoid of passions, devoid of impulses, free from spontaneity. This cold creature that will never feel drawn to its peers by love and sympathy but will access necessary production relationships determined by economic need; this human machine that will not know dreams, ideals, ambition, hate, struggle, but will join others to fill its belly and make life comfortable; this

ENZO MARTUCCI

ugly contraption that will have no thoughts and ideas other than those that are suited to its material interests and inspired by the stomach; will be the citizen of the future, the champion of the gray Marxist world. He will move beyond good and evil, not in the sense of abandoning the various and opposite tendencies of the soul and human nature, but in the most monstrous sense of the lack of any psychic tendency, any soul, any nature. He will be the representative of a life reduced to pure physiology and the incarnation of an amoralism deriving not from the recognition of different actions and valuations, but from the reality of a single action and valuation, in a humanity frighteningly equal, in general brutishness.

To realize, in the near future, this mechanical and insensitive type, communist morality immediately creates another type that will pave the way for the first: the fanatical and bloody beast, thirsty for domination and eager to take over the world by any means, with slaughter and slander, lies and hypocrisy. Bolshevism must precede Marxism, and the theocracy of the red priests must prepare for the unnaturalization of mankind over which it can better reign. When man is reduced to a puppet without feelings or will, a machine that will need only lubricant, the Bolshevik oligarchy will dominate eternally without fearing revolt.

From today until then, violence and flattery, perversion and illusions, to bend nature. And the goal will be achieved. *Cavat gutta lapidem.*[34]

---

34   A drop hollows out a stone.

Many people, enticed by the earthly paradise that communism promises, gather around its banner without realizing that social hedonism and the general harmony of the future city will, in practice, be identified with the passivity and inertia of *pieces of wood* used despotically by the triumphant beast and arbitrarily arranged in the absurd disposition of an artificial and tyrannical order. The crowds, almost always, reject sincere ideas that do not promise chimerical happiness, do not renounce struggle and pain and seek to improve life within the limits of the possible; instead, they are attracted by those other ideas, shining and false, that deceive with the mirage of Eden where freedom is not conquered but obtained without effort, where peace reigns supreme and well-being and joy delight everyone.

Men, fascinated by illusion, resemble prisoners in the cave that Plato recalls in Book Seven of the *Republic*: chained in the desire for the Golden Age, they cannot turn around and look at the reality of which they see only the shadow on the wall in front of them. The masses, deceived by the shepherds and drunk with plenty, consider the promises of demagoguery as achievable goals and precipitate into the abyss at the moment they believe they are touching the ultimate end, the definitive purpose, the point of convergence of love and pleasure. They do not know what Dostoevsky teaches, namely that "in life itself, and not in the thing to be attained, which must always be expressed as a formula, as positive as twice two makes four, and such positiveness is not life,

ENZO MARTUCCI

gentlemen, but is the beginning of death."[35]

Bolshevism aims to destroy the old civilization, not to replace it with a new civilization or with heroic barbarism like that of the Odinic saga, but rather with a flat, vile, and nauseating barbarism. The future era that it promises to humanity is nothing but the era of the *last man*, whom Zarathustra speaks of with disdain, and in which everything is shrunk, castrated, and made swinish. And it is this kingdom of pigs, this mechanical world where one lives only to eat, that stupid crowds invoke, believing that it will bring the new earthly paradise, the beneficial triumph of brotherhood and freedom.

But fortunately, there are still a few men who feel the pride and beauty of life and value the bitter joy of struggle more than the soft beatitude of quietness. And to these men, I launch my war cry: Let us crush Bolshevism! Let us crush false and hypocritical eudemonism! Let us destroy the lie of universal good! Let life become ever greater and more heroic, tumultuous and protean, an eternal source of the unexpected, a fertile matrix of novelties!

In the twilight of the old bourgeois and timid world, on the ruins of the idols consecrated by the cowardice of the masses, we will hail the death of the red beast, repeating with Nietzsche:

> We philosophers and "free spirits" feel ourselves irradiated as by a new dawn by the report

---

35   Fyodor Dostoyevsky, translated by Constance Garnett, *Notes from Underground*, London: Heinemann, 1918.

that the "old God is dead"; our hearts overflow with gratitude, astonishment, presentiment and expectation. At last the horizon seems open once more, granting even that it is not bright; our ships can at last put out to sea in face of every danger; every hazard is again permitted to the discerner; the sea, our sea, again lies open before us; perhaps never before did such an "open sea" exist.[36]

36   F. Nietzsche, *The Gay Science,* Translated by Thomas Common, New York: Macmillan 1911.

POSTSCRIPTUM

A professor friend who was seduced by the immaculate purity of Picasso's dove and is a member of the Peace Partisans Movement wanted to read the manuscript of this book before I handed it over to the printer. Then he told me:

> I advise you not to publish. Even if what you claim is true, it's best that the people don't know about it. Otherwise, they would lose faith in the Communist Party, which is the only party that can change the situation in Italy and give us something new. And we would remain under the weight of the bourgeois society for who knows how long. And you would contribute, albeit involuntarily, to maintaining the current state of affairs. Besides, to an immoralist like you, a ruthless person, a chaos advocate, the practice of violence and hypocrisy that the communists have been forced to resort to in order to gain power should not be a horror to you.

I respond to my professor friend.

I will publish!

And for the following reasons.

I am an enemy of bourgeois society and, through 32 years of struggle, I have tried to strike it in every way.

But I don't want to jump out of the frying pan into the fire.

I do not intend to prepare the ground for the advent of a tyranny worse than all those that humanity has endured to date. And so, while I fight the current world, I say to the oppressed:

"Get rid of the bosses but do not create others, more cruel and exploitative. Destroy the present but refrain from building a future based on statism."

Why do I say this?

For a very simple reason.

Namely, the instinctive disgust that inspires me that monstrous mixture of Mongolian barbarism and standardized automation that characterizes the Soviet world and that Italian Bolsheviks would like to bring to us as well. Precisely to us, who by nature, tradition, and sentiment, are absolutely reluctant to be treated like sheep that, gregariously, follow the Tartar shepherd or like wheels that, mechanically, mesh into the social machinery.

The professor friend will remind me that the Latin people have degenerated, no longer have the romantic spirit and the sense of personality that they had in the past.

Agreed. However, as much as we have decayed, we are not yet so much that we can tolerate the whip of Little Father Stalin.

And the new that Bolshevism would give us, would be felt by us as a much heavier chain than the one inflicted on our fathers by the Goths of Theodoric or the Lombards of Alboin.

That is why I am opposed to Bolshevism.

Because I do not want Italy to become, like Russia, a horrible barracks in which men and women will be forced to mark time, singing the praises of the motorized Tamerlane.

Because I do not want the Italian people to be reduced to a gray mass of puppets who cannot think with their brains, feel with their hearts, and walk with their legs, but must understand, feel, and act in the only way that the red leaders will establish.

Because I do not like what happens to the Italian worker, which happens today to the Russian worker who, if he arrives five minutes late to the factory, is locked up in it for six months, cannot leave, cannot receive visitors, and after working hours, must remain segregated in special rooms where he eats and sleeps.[37]

Because I don't consider it human that workers are denied the right to strike, the possibility of demanding economic improvement. This happens in the Soviet Union where the State—the only capitalist—owns all the means of production and requires the proletarians to make them profitable for

---

37   Soviet labor legislation stipulates that a worker who arrives late to the factory three times must be confined there for six months. If, after this punishment, he continues to arrive late, he is assigned to a concentration camp as a "production saboteur." [ENZO]

its exclusive interest. In exchange, the State pays the proletarians the miserable salary that it itself sets and that the proletarians must accept without discussing, without saying a word, if they do not want to end up in forced labor in Siberia, where they die of hunger, cold, and lashes. So the workers languish in hunger and the State—which identifies with the Communist Party—absorbs all the wealth and uses it to maintain many hierarchs who lead the life of nabobs, a huge army, a formidable police force, a gigantic bureaucracy, a swarm of spies, in short, an infinity of parasites who live behind and with the sweat of workers and peasants. This happens in Russia and will also happen in Italy if the little Khan Togliatti governs it on behalf of the great Khan Stalin.

And here, by analogy, I recall an episode.

One day, in 1949, I heard a speech given to the partisans in Incisa Valdarno by Hon. Walter Audisio, otherwise known as "Colonel Valerio." This gentleman sympathized with the fate of poor Italian proletarians, forced to emigrate to Argentina and work in wild lands where, he said, "no man's foot has ever set foot." Listening to him, I immediately thought that the Colonel, as good and charitable as he was, was trying to use not only his hands and feet but also his brain and all the other organs at his disposal to reduce Italian workers and intellectuals to the same conditions as Russian workers and intellectuals who, guilty only of having thought with their heads, are condemned to dig large navigable canals, under the whip of the tormentors and the snowstorms, with

ENZO MARTUCCI

hunger cramps that grip the stomach and nostalgia for freedom that torments the soul.

All these delights the Bolshevik gentlemen would like to transplant in Italy. And I, who deeply feel horror about it, oppose their action even though, in doing so, I contribute to keeping the bourgeois society alive, as the professor judges.

Valentin Gonzales, known as El Campesino, who was a hero of the Spanish resistance against Franco and who later, as a reward, received from Stalin the accusation of deviationism and was assigned to confinement, when he managed to escape, published what he saw in Russia. And, among other things, he said that the millions of soldiers who, repelling the Germans, had occupied the regions of Central Europe, after the war did not return to their homes. But they ended up in concentration camps where they would die. And this was to prevent them from being able to tell in their countries what they had seen, namely that there is less slavery in capitalist nations than in the Soviet Union and a better treatment for the working class. This is the Bolshevik paradise! This is the wonderful Eden that Don Palmiro and Don Pietro take as a model! And this is also the new one that the seraphic professor is willing to accept in order to immediately have another society that, perhaps, will allow him advancement in his... career. But I, who have no career to follow; I, who have always paid personally and out of my own pocket, remaining faithful to my feelings and ideas; I, who have openly opposed the bourgeoisie, throwing open the door to the prison and confinement, while others remained prudently hidden behind the comfortable chair of a provincial high school; I say no to Bolshevism. And I shout this no with all the strength of my lungs, without caring about the scandalized judgment of the professor who will label me reactionary, or sold to De Gasperi, or corrupted by the dollars of an American banker.

The professor declares: "An immoralist, an unscrupulous person, a supporter of chaos should not feel horror for the practice of violence and the use of hypocrisy followed by communists to gain power."

I immediately respond as an unscrupulous and immoralist. And I assert: I have gone beyond the rusty gates of Good and Evil. But, despite this, I have my preferences. Certain things I like and certain things disgust me. Therefore, it is natural that I seek to achieve what I like and fight against what nauseates me. Even if I consider everything equivalent, with respect to nature, in whose bosom there are no qualitative distinctions.

As an aesthete, I understand and admire the crime of Corrado Brando in D'Annunzio's tragedy *Più Che l'Amore*. I exalt the heroism of the anarchist bandit Giulio Bonnot, who robs banks and falls in the fight with a gun in his hand. All of this is sympathetic to me because it expresses strength, courage, and daring. But even if I do not objectively condemn it, even if I consider it possible for beings different from me, to whom nature has spared sensitivity, I feel disgust for those manifestations that reveal cowardice, simulation, perfidy. And, in defense of the eagle, I fight the snake. Even if, with Zarathustra, I think that both the eagle and the snake are necessary for the universal reality.

Furthermore, balance arises from struggle. And the reaction of the *generous madmen*, if it can never suppress ferocity, can prevent it from becoming the *sole means of governance*. And that innocent women and children are tortured and killed only because a relative who is hated by Stalin has fled abroad, escaping the clutches of the red police. Like what happened to the daughter of the Russian anarchist Pukov, whom I met in Paris, to whom the executioners of the GPU ripped off the pubic hair, twisted the breasts, used carnal violence, and finally set her on fire after pouring gasoline on her.

The small bourgeois professor calls me a "supporter of chaos." I observe: from chaos comes balance. From balance, we return to chaos. And vice versa. But why does this happen?

Therefore, the elements need cohesion, but then they feel the need for dissociation when the cohesion becomes too tight and suffocating. Each peculiarity wants to remain itself and, in order not to be crushed by the others, develops its energy to the maximum and contains the adverse forces of the neighboring elements. So there is life for all.

Among men, it is the same. The ties of society

generate the need to break free; but, once freed, individuals must squeeze their personality, extract all their power, to contain the overflow of other personalities that seek to dominate. And then one stops the other, but all remain with a vast field to assert themselves and enjoy. Those who do not know how to become strong, die; but they fall heroically, in an attempt to conquer the entire life. And those who remain can finally intoxicate themselves with the ambrosia of the superman and the nepenthe of the unique.

This philosophy may be judged immoral, monstrous, diabolical, but no one can deny it the merit of spurring individuals to shake off laziness or resignation and to develop all personal energies in view of a full and tumultuous existence. Therefore, it could be defined as the *philosophy of individuation*.

Instead, the philosophy that the Bolsheviks teach could be called the philosophy of diminishment. It tells man: "You are nothing and can do nothing alone. You must always be with others and make yourself equal to them. You and the others must recognize the rule of the leaders who make your union profitable and allow it to function. All leaders must, in turn, depend on the supreme leader, Stalin, the embodiment of the triad: wisdom, power, goodness. Therefore, Stalin is God. The human individual is less than manure."

The professor who drinks chamomile every evening and accompanies his wife to Sunday Mass, despite not believing in the Christian Father and preferring, in his worship, the Moscow idol, can accept the theory of the fanatics of the cells, the catechism, naive and barbaric, which deifies the assassin of 20 million Slavs and denies the creative possibility of the self.

But those who, like me, are "chaos supporters" and sworn enemies of every prison and barracks, spit on the filthy ant colony that, under the scorching snows, hides Cayenne, and prepare the bombs that, destroying Bolshevism, will save life and avenge freedom.

ENZO MARTUCCI
January 1953

ALSO AVAILABLE:

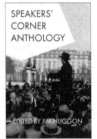